D1170650

Zanzibar
& Pemba

Sue Watt & Lizzie Williams

Credits

Footprint credits

Editor: Alan Murphy
Production and layout: Angus Dawson
Maps: Kevin Feeney

Managing Director: Andy Riddle
Commercial Director: Patrick Dawson
Publisher: Alan Murphy
Publishing Managers: Felicity Laughton, Nicola Gibbs
Digital Editors: Jo Williams, Tom Mellors
Marketing and PR: Liz Harper
Sales: Diane McEntee
Advertising: Renu Sibal
Finance and Administration: Elizabeth Taylor

Photography credits

Front cover: Jonathan Tichon/Shutterstock
Back cover: Vlad Ageshin/Shutterstock

Printed in Great Britain by CPI Antony Rowe, Chippenham, Wiltshire

Every effort has been made to ensure that the facts in this guidebook are accurate. However, travellers should still obtain advice from consulates, airlines, etc about travel and visa requirements before travelling. The authors and publishers cannot accept responsibility for any loss, injury or inconvenience however caused.

MIX
Paper from responsible sources
FSC® C013604
www.fsc.org

Publishing information

Footprint *Focus Zanzibar & Pemba*
1st edition
© Footprint Handbooks Ltd
August 2011

ISBN: 978 1 908206 18 3
CIP DATA: A catalogue record for this book is available from the British Library

® Footprint Handbooks and the Footprint mark are a registered trademark of Footprint Handbooks Ltd

Published by Footprint
6 Riverside Court
Lower Bristol Road
Bath BA2 3DZ, UK
T +44 (0)1225 469141
F +44 (0)1225 469461
www.footprinttravelguides.com

Distributed in the USA by Globe Pequot Press, Guilford, Connecticut

The content of Footprint *Focus Zanzibar & Pemba* has been taken directly from Footprint's *Tanzania Handbook* which was researched and written by Lizzie Williams and Sue Watt, based on the *East Africa Handbook*, which was written by Michael Hodd and Angela Roche.

Contents

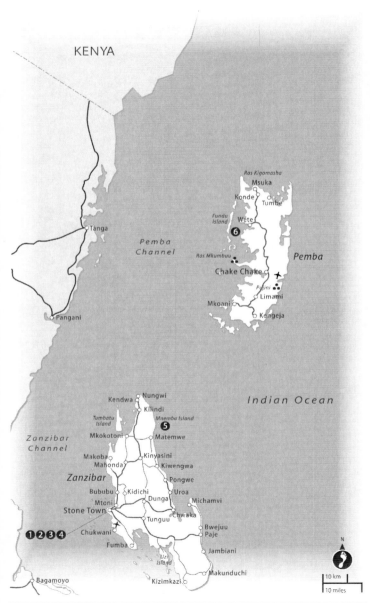

KENYA

Ras Kigomasha
Msuka
Konde · Tumbe
Fundu Island · Wete
⑥
Pemba Channel
Ras Mkumbuu · ·
Chake Chake ✈
Pemba
Tanga
Pujini · ·
Limami
Mkoani · Kengeja
Pangani

Indian Ocean

Kendwa · Nungwi
Kilindi
Tumbatu Island _Mnemba Island_
⑤
Mkokotoni · Matemwe
Zanzibar Channel
Makoba · Kinyasini
Mahonda · Kiwengwa
Zanzibar · Pongwe
Bububu · Kidichi · Uroa
Mtoni · Dunga · Michamvi
Stone Town ✈ · Chwaka
①②③④ Chukwani · Tunguu
Fumba · Bwejuu
Paje
Uzi Island · Jambiani
Kizimkazi · Makunduchi
Bagamoyo

N

10 km
10 miles

The very name Zanzibar conjures up exotic and romantic images. The main town on Zanzibar Island, Stone Town, with its intriguing, winding alleyways, old Arabian townhouses and heaving port, is steeped in history, full of atmosphere and immensely attractive. Zanzibar's coastlines offer some of the best beaches in the world, but sand and surf vary depending on what side of the island you're on. On the east coast, waves break over coral reefs and sand bars offshore, and low tide reveals small pools of starfish. Up north, ocean swimming is much less susceptible to the tides, and smooth beaches and white sand make for dazzling days in the sun. Roads to the southeast coast take visitors through the Jozani Forest, home to Zanzibar's rare red colobus monkeys and a number of other primate and small antelope species. But Zanzibar attracts hundreds of thousands of visitors a year, and to some extent the island has suffered from the consequences of over-zealous mass tourism. In recent years its popularity as a European charter destination has seen the growth of all-inclusive resorts housing tourists on sun, sea and sand holidays, from where visitors experience little of the island outside the compound of their resort.

Quite by contrast, Pemba is hardly visited at all and is infinitely more difficult to get around. The sea around Pemba is dotted with desert islands and is the location of some of the best scuba-diving in the Indian Ocean. The Pemba Channel drops off steeply just off the west coast and the diverse species of marine life and coral are exceptional. Unlike Zanzibar, tourism is still in its early stages and a visit here is truly a Robinson Crusoe experience.

Planning your trip

Getting there

Air → *See also Airport information, below, and Transport in Dar es Salaam, page 51.*

The majority of travellers arrive in Tanzania through Dar es Salaam's **Julius Nyerere International Airport** (JNIA). There are also direct international flights to **Zanzibar** (see page 56). There is a departure tax of US$50 (US$25 from Zanzibar) on all international flights leaving Tanzanian airports but this is usually included in the price of the ticket. When flying to Tanzania, getting a window seat is definitely a good option, as cloud permitting, you may be lucky enough to get a glimpse of the gleaming top of Mount Kilimanjaro. It is not generally cheaper to arrange a return to Nairobi and a connecting return flight to Dar es Salaam. But for travellers who are only visiting the northern circuit parks, it is easier to fly to Nairobi, given that Arusha is only 273 km to the south of Nairobi, and enter Tanzania through the Namanga land border from Kenya. There are regular shuttle buses between Nairobi and Arusha and Moshi (see box, page 11). You can also fly from Nairobi to Kilimanjaro (for more information, see Getting around, page 8). Nairobi is served by more airlines than Dar es Salaam so air fares are more competitively priced.

Airport information

Julius Nyerere International Airport ① *T022-284 4212, www.jnia.aero*, is in Kipawa, 13 km or a half an hour's drive southwest of Dar es Salaam along Nyerere Road. There are foreign exchange bureaux, one bank, two ATMs, car hire facilities, a post office, duty free shop and a bar and restaurant. Flight information is virtually impossible to obtain by telephone at the airport, contact the airline directly. Airline offices are listed under Dar es Salaam, page 51, and Arusha, page . Phone cards are available from shops at the airport and cost US$4. There are public telephones in the terminal buildings. Some of the more upmarket hotels can arrange a shuttle service to and from the airport, which must be booked in advance. There are private buses (*dala-dala*), which cost about US$1 but are very crowded and it's a five minute walk out to Nyerere Road to catch one, which is a hassle with luggage. A taxi to town will cost US$25-35 depending on your destination and traffic conditions. Check with the information desk in the airport what you should be paying, before negotiating with a taxi driver. If you are going directly to Zanzibar, you can either enquire at the airport about the next flight, or it takes about 30 minutes to drive from the airport to the ferry terminal in the city.

Zanzibar International Airport ① *T024-223 3979, www.zanzibar-airport.com*, is 7 km southwest of Stone Town. On arrival you will be badgered by the taxi drivers. Ask inside the airport what you should pay for the short taxi ride into town, this will help with the bargaining once outside. A taxi should cost in the region of US$6-10, or alternatively there are *dala-dala* from the traffic island outside of the airport to Creek Road in town for less than US$1. Some of the more upmarket hotels and resorts offer airport pick ups, so it is always worthwhile asking and these should cost in the region of US$30 into town and US$65 to the coastal resorts for four to six people. There are forex bureaux at the airport immediately before you exit the baggage retrieval area, and the rates are competitive.

Don't miss ...

Road

If you are **driving**, border crossings between Tanzania and its neighbours can be laborious or simple, depending on your preparation and the state of your vehicle's paperwork. You will require a Carnet de Passage issued by a body in your own country (such as the Automobile Association), vehicle registration, and you will also be required to take out third party insurance for Tanzania from one of the insurance companies who have kiosks at the border posts. Travelling in a car registered in Kenya requires leaving the vehicle log book with the Kenyan customs, (keeping a photocopy for the Tanzanian side), and you'll be issued with a temporary export permit that is valid for three months. Tanzania charges US$90 for the car (multiple entry valid for three months). Most car hire companies will not allow you to take a rented vehicle out of Tanzania, but some may consider it if you only want to go to Kenya.

From Kenya The main road crossing is at Namanga, about halfway along the road between Arusha and Nairobi. As this border receives thousands of tourists on safari each week en route between the Kenyan and Tanzanian parks it is reasonably quick and efficient. There are also regular shuttle buses (see box, page 11) connecting the two cities, which take about six to seven hours on fairly good roads all the way (the Arusha–Namanga stretch is currently being re-tarred). A cheaper alternative is to do the journey in stages by taking a minibus from Ronald Ngala Road in Nairobi to Namanga, crossing the border on foot, and then catching another minibus to Arusha. This will take a little longer than the shuttle, but will cost half the price. Other crossings are at Lunga Lunga, see page , between Mombasa and Dar es Salaam on a recently improved road. There are daily through buses between the two cities. Public buses and minibuses (*dala-dalas*) frequent the quieter border crossings at Taveta, between Moshi and Voi, at Isebania, and between Kisuma and Musoma. Visas for both Tanzania and Kenya are available at all the borders.

Other neighbouring countries Travellers entering Tanzania from **Malawi** will pass through the Songwe border southeast of Mbeya. There are bus services between Lilongwe and Dar es Salaam, and services between Lilongwe, Mzuzu and Mbeya depart several times each week. Most nationalities do not require a visa for Malawi. Until recently getting to Tanzania from **Mozambique** was fairly limited, as there were no bridges over the Ruvuma River and the only option was a car ferry at Mtwara, which sank in 2008 and can still be seen in the middle of the river at low tide. However, this is set to change as the 720 m Unity Bridge is presently under construction. Tanzania and Mozambique are splitting the US$24 million price tag and the Chinese are building it. It will connect southern Tanzania at Masuguru

Village with northern Mozambique at Negonane Village in the Cabo Delgado Province, which is about 200 km from the coast and will be accessed in Tanzania by a new tarred road from Lindi. Those without vehicles can cross by passenger boat at Kilambo, south of Mtwara. It is essential to have a visa for Mozambique which can be arranged at the embassy in Dar es Salaam (see page 54). There is a good bus link to the border with **Rwanda** at Rusomo, although those in private vehicles must be aware that there have been incidents of banditry on the roads to the southwest of Lake Victoria. This is roughly 170 km on a fairly good road from Rwanda's capital of Kigali which is served by regular minibuses. Rwandan visas, for those who need them, are available at the border. There are buses leaving very early each day from Ngala, 10 km from the border post on the Tanzania side, and arriving at Mwanza in the evening. Minibuses link the border with Ngala, where there is a clutch of basic board and lodgings if you need to stay overnight, which you may need to do if you are coming from the Kigali direction and have to wait for the buses on the following morning. From **Uganda** there is crossing at Mutukulu, northwest of Bukoba, but this is a rough road and the only option is to hitch, though minibuses do run from the Ugandan side of the border to Masaka. Unless you are in the extreme northwest of Tanzania anyway, the easiest way to get from Tanzania to Uganda is via Nairobi (Kenya). Scandinavia Express has buses from Dar via Arusha to Nairobi and on to Kampala. There are buses to the border with **Zambia** at Nakonde, see page . You have to walk between the border posts (or use a bicycle-taxi) to Tunduma where there are buses to Mbeya. Visas are available at the Ugandan and Zambian borders.

Overland trucks

Overland truck safaris are a popular way of exploring Tanzania by road. They demand a little more fortitude and adventurous spirit from the traveller, but the compensation is usually the camaraderie and life-long friendships that result from what is invariably a real adventure, going to places the more luxurious travellers will never visit. The standard overland route most commercial trucks take through East Africa (in either direction) is from Nairobi a two-week circuit into Uganda to see the mountain gorillas via some of the Kenya national parks, then crossing into Tanzania to Arusha for the Ngorongoro Crater and Serengeti, before heading south to Dar es Salaam, for Zanzibar. If you have more time, you can complete the full circuit that goes from Tanzania through Malawi and Zambia to Livingstone to see the Victoria Falls, and then another three weeks from there to Cape Town in South Africa via Botswana and Namibia. There are several overland companies with departures almost weekly from Nairobi, Dar es Salaam, Livingstone and Cape Town.

Getting around

Air → *See also Transport in Dar es Salaam, page 51.*
Air Tanzania has a limited schedule of domestic flights between Dar, Zanzibar, Mwanza and Kilimanjaro. But the state-owned carrier has suffered from severe financial and operating difficulties recently, meaning that flights are cancelled and the schedules change all the time. The private airlines offer a much more extensive air coverage of the country and there are 62 airports and airstrips managed by the Tanzania Airports Authority (TAA). **Precision Air** has flights from Arusha, Kilimanjaro, Dar es Salaam, Tabora, Kigoma, Mwanza, Bukoba, Lindi, Mtwara, Grumeti and Seronera in the Serengeti National

Park and Zanzibar and also connects with Nairobi. Sample one way fares are Dar-Zanzibar, from US$70; Pemba–Dar, from US$120: and Mwanza–Dar, from US$480. The smaller companies, **Air Excel**, **Regional Air**, **Zan Air** and **Coastal Air** run flights between Dar es Salaam, Zanzibar, Arusha and to the various smaller regional airports and national park airstrips such as Grumeti, Mafia, Lake Manyara, Pemba, Ruaha, Rubondo, Selous, Seronera, and Tanga. **Regional Air**, code shares with **Air Kenya**, so also has flights between Dar, Kilimanjaro and Zanzibar and Nairobi. **Air Excel**, code shares with **Safarilink**, in Kenya so also has a service between Kilimanjaro and Nairobi. These airlines use small six- or 12-seater planes and have frequent scheduled flights but will only fly with the required minimum of passengers, though sometimes this is only two people. Note that on the smaller aircraft, the baggage allowance is 15 kg so you may have to leave luggage at hotels in Dar or Arusha, which most will allow you to for a small fee. Specific schedules are detailed under each relevant chapter.

Air charter Several companies offer small planes for charter, especially between the parks and islands, and have flights most days of the week. These can work out to be economical for groups of 4-6 people, and some companies offer scenic flights.

Dar es Salaam: **Flightlink**, T022-284 2280, www.flightlinkaircharters.com, and **Zantas Air**, T022-213 7181, www.zantasair.com; Mwanza: **Renair**, T028-256 0403, www.ren air.com; Kilimanjaro: **Kilimanjaro Air Safaris**, T027-275 0523, www.kiliair.com.

Rail → *See also Transport in Dar es Salaam, page 53.*

There are two railway companies operating in Tanzania. **TAZARA** ① *T022-226 2191, www.tazara.co.tz*, is the name of the Tanzania-Zambia Railway Authority and the trains run from Dar es Salaam, southwest to Zambia (see Getting there, above). The other service is the **Tanzania Railway Corporation** ① *T022-211 7833, www.trctz.com*, which operates services between Dar es Salam and Kigoma with a branch line to Mwanza. The Northern line service to Tanga and Moshi has been discontinued. There are three classes of travel; first class compartment sleeping two, second class compartment sleeping six, and third class sitting. The latter gets very uncomfortable and crowded and you'll be sitting among piles of boxes and live chickens. All cabins on Tanzanian trains are sexually segregated unless you book the whole cabin. While the trains themselves are a little grubby, and more than a little infested by cockroaches, the bedding is very clean. It is essential to guard your possessions fiercely and keep cabin doors locked at all times. In fact you'll be given a piece of wood to wedge into the window to prevent anyone from opening it from the outside at night when the trains pull into stations. The trains have dining cars, which turn into rowdy bars late at night, and each first and second class carriage has a steward who can deliver a plate of adequate chicken and rice or *ugali* and beef or similar, which you can eat in your compartment. The better option really, so you don't have to leave your luggage. In the morning the steward comes round with tea and coffee and the trains stop for a while at a trackside village for breakfast, when the enterprising villagers set up a row of stalls of street food next to the train.

Road → *See also Transport in Dar es Salaam, page 52.*

Bus There is now an efficient network of privately run buses across the country. On good sealed roads, buses cover 50-80 km per hour. On unsealed or poorly maintained roads they will average only 20 km per hour. Larger buses give a considerably more comfortable ride than minibuses and have more space for luggage, and are to be recommended on safety grounds as well. If you are taking a shorter journey (Dar–Morogoro or Mwanza– Musoma, say), the bus will leave when full. You can join an almost full bus and leave promptly for an uncomfortable journey, either standing or on a makeshift gangway seat. Or you can secure a comfortable seat and wait until the bus fills, which can take one or two hours on a less busy route. If you are making a long journey you can book a seat at kiosks run by the bus companies at the bus stations. On the larger and more travelled routes (Dar–Arusha, Dar–Mbeya, Dar–Mombasa in Kenya) there is now a choice of 'luxury', 'semi-luxury' and 'ordinary', and fares vary by a few dollars. The difference between them is that the 'luxury' and 'semi-luxury' buses often have air conditioning and only take the number of people the buses are designed to seat. On the 'ordinary' services, the buses are usually older, carry additional standing passengers and stop more frequently en route, making the journey considerably slower. Fares on all buses are very reasonable, for example on a 'luxury' bus the fare from Arusha to Dar es Salaam (a journey of 650 km or eight hours) is around US$18, on a semi-luxury bus it's US$11, and on an ordinary bus US$9. On the main routes it is possible to book ahead at a kiosk at the bus stand and this is wise rather than turning up at the departure time on the off-chance. Consistently recommended is **Scandinavia Express**, which has its own terminal in Dar es Salaam, T022-218 4833, www.scandinaviagroup.com. They are very popular so book ahead when possible, the offices throughout the country issue computerized tickets, and you can choose your seat on screen. Buses are speed limited, luggage is securely locked up either under the bus or in overhead compartments, and complimentary video, drinks, sweets and biscuits are offered. On long journeys on the main highways, the buses stop at roadside restaurants for lunch.

Car Driving is on the left side of the road. The key roads are in good condition, and there has been considerable road-building going on in Tanzania in recent years thanks to foreign aid. The best roads are the tarmac ones from Dar es Salaam to Zambia and Malawi, Dar es Salaam to Arusha and the new tarred road from Arusha to the Ngorongoro Crater. The road from Arusha to the Kenyan border at Namanga is presently being re-tarred. Away from the main highways, however, the majority of roads are bad and hazardous. Most of the minor roads are unmade gravel with potholes: there are many rough stretches and they deteriorate further in the rainy season. Road conditions in the reserves and national parks of Tanzania are extremely rough. During the rainy season, many roads are passable only with high clearance 4WD vehicles. Fuel is available along the main highways and towns, but if you're going way off the beaten track, consider taking a couple of jerry cans of extra fuel. Also ensure the vehicle has a jack and possibly take a shovel to dig it out of mud or sand. If you break down, it is common practice in Tanzania to place a bundle of leaves 50 m or so before and behind the vehicle to warn oncoming motorists.

Car hire Most people visit the national parks on an organized safari, but if you're confident driving in Tanzania, there is also the option to hire a car. Car hire is not as well organized in Tanzania as it is in Kenya. There are fewer companies (although this is changing) and they are more expensive. Also, many of the vehicles are poorly maintained and you may find it difficult to hire a car without a driver. In saying that however, by contrast to the rest of the country, hiring a Suzuki jeep on Zanzibar is a popular way to explore the island. To hire a car

Kenya–Tanzania shuttle services

Shuttle buses run daily between Kenya and Tanzania; Nairobi (city centre)–Nairobi Jomo Kenyatta International Airport–Arusha (via the Namanga border post)–Kilimanjaro International Airport–Moshi. There is an early morning and early afternoon departure, and expect to pay about US$30 for Nairobi to Arusha, US$40 for Nairobi to Moshi, and US$20 from Kilimanjaro International Airport to Arusha or Moshi. The journey time from Nairobi to Arusha is 6½ hours and it's another 1½ hours to Moshi via the airport. The company websites have booking facilities, timetables, prices and where to meet the buses. At the border drivers will assist passengers with formalities.

AA Shuttles, www.aashuttles.com.
Bobby Tours, www.bobbytours.com.
Impala Shuttles, www.impalashuttle.com.
Riverside Shuttles, www.riverside-shuttle.com.

you generally need to be over 23, have an international driving licence, or pay a small fee to have your own country licence endorsed in Tanzania, and to leave a large deposit or sign a blank credit card voucher. Always take out the collision damage waiver premium as even the smallest accident can be very expensive, although you'll still be liable of an excess of around US$500-1000. Also consider taking out a theft protection waiver. Costs vary between the different car hire companies and are from around US$60-80 per day for a normal saloon car or a jeep on Zanzibar, rising to US$120-180 for a 4WD. Deals can be made for more than seven days' car hire. Finally, Tanzania's rather hefty 20% VAT is added to all costs. It is essential to shop around and ask questions of the companies about what is and what is not included in the rates. On safari you will have to pay the park entrance fees for the car and the driver, if you have one, and although it will work out expensive this method does allow for greater flexibility than an organized safari. Most of the tour and travel agents listed in the book will be able to arrange vehicle hire.

Dala-dala Called *dala-dala*, it is said, because they charged a dollar, although this seems a high sum, these are local private buses and passenger vehicles using Toyota (or other) minibuses. On Zanzibar they are also made from small trucks. They are by the far largest method of urban and rural transport and are cheap, US$0.30 for a short journey, rising to US$0.50 for a longer one. However they get very crowded and there is often a squeeze to get on. But fellow travellers will be very helpful in directing you to the correct *dala-dala* if you ask (most have a sign indicating their route and destination on the front), will advise on connections, fight on your behalf to try to get you a seat and tell you when to get off at your destination. Many *dala-dala*, have inspirational messages on the front and back windows like 'God is Great', 'Viva Manchester United', or (rather ominously) 'Still Alive'.

Taxis Hotels and town centre locations are well served by taxis, some good and some very run-down but serviceable. It is wise to sit in the back if there are no front seat belts. Hotel staff, even at the smallest locations, will rustle up a taxi even when there is not one waiting outside. If you visit an out-of-town centre location, it is wise to ask the taxi to wait – it will normally be happy to do so for benefit of the return fare. A short trip in the centre of Dar es Salaam should cost about US$3-4, while a longer trip to the outskirts of the city such as the university (13 km) would be about US$8-10. There is a bargaining element: none of the cabs have meters, and you should establish the fare (*bei gani?* – how much?) before you set off. Prices are generally fair as drivers simply won't take you if you offer a fare that's too low. A common practice is a driver will set off and *then* go and get petrol using part of your fare to pay for it, so often the first part of a journey is spent sitting in a petrol station. Also be aware that seemingly taxi drivers *never* have change, so try and accumulate some small notes for taxi rides.

Tuk-tuks These motorized three-wheel buggies are starting to feature in many of African cities and are cheap and convenient. The driver sits in the front whilst two or three passengers can sit comfortably on the back seat. They offer a service that is at least half the price of regular taxis. They do not, however, go very fast so for longer journeys stick to taxis. In Tanzania they are known as *Bajajis*, after the Bajaj Auto Company that manufactures many of them.

Sea and lake Between Dar es Salaam and Zanzibar there are several sailings each day on modern hydrofoils and an older ferry (see page 52 for details). These are reliable and pleasant and on the newer ones movies are shown and refreshments are available.

Sleeping

There is a wide range of accommodation on offer from top-of-the-range lodges and tented camps that charge US$300-1000 per couple per day, to mid-range safari lodges and beach resorts with double rooms with air conditioning and bathroom for around US$150-250, standard and faded small town hotels used by local business people for around US$50-100 per room, and basic board and lodgings used by local travellers at under US$10 a day. At the top end of the market, Tanzania now boasts some accommodation options that would rival the luxurious camps in southern Africa – intimate safari camps with unrivalled degrees of comfort and service in stunning settings. The beach resorts too have improved considerably in recent years, and there are some highly luxurious and romantic beach lodges and hotels that again are in commanding positions

Generally, accommodation booked through a European agent will be more expensive than if you contact the hotel or lodge directly. Tanzania's hoteliers are embracing the age of the internet, and an ever-increasing number can take a reservation by email or through their websites. Low season in East Africa is generally around the long rainy season from the beginning of April to the end of June, when most room rates drop considerably. Some even close during this time, though the resorts on Zanzibar stay open throughout the year.

For the more expensive hotels, the airlines, and game park entrance and camping fees, a system operates whereby tourists are charged approximately double the local rate and this must be paid in foreign currency and not TSh. In the cheaper hotels you should get away with paying in TSh but always ask before checking in.

Hotels

Most town and city hotels tend to be bland with poor service, but increasingly, much nicer options are opening outside the major towns. For instance, many guesthouses have opened up on coffee farms around Arusha. In some areas, Stone Town on Zanzibar being the prime example, there is the opportunity to sleep in some historical and atmospheric hotels. Here, even the cheaper establishments are beautiful old houses decorated with fine antiques and Persian carpets, with traditional Zanzibar four-poster beds swathed in mosquito nets.

Sleeping and eating price codes

Sleeping

$$$$ over US$300   **$$$** US$100-300   **$$** US$50-100
$ under US$30

Prices include taxes and service charge, but not meals. They are based on a double room, except in the **$** range, where prices are almost always per person.

Eating

¶¶¶ over US$30   **¶¶** US$15-30   **¶** under US$15

Prices refer to the cost of a two-course meal, not including drinks.

At the budget end there's a fairly wide choice of cheap accommodation. A room often comprises a simple bed, shared toilet and washing facilities, and may have an irregular water supply; it is always a good idea to look at a room before deciding, to ensure it's clean and everything works. Check that mosquito nets are provided. It is also imperative to ensure that your luggage will be locked away securely for protection against petty theft. At the very bottom of the budget scale are numerous basic lodgings in all the towns that cost under US$10. For this you get a bare room with a bed and a door that may or may not lock. Unless these are exceptionally secure or good value, they are generally not recommended and are often simply rooms attached to a bar that, more often than not, are rented by the hour.

Note that the word 'hotel' (or in Swahili, *hoteli*) means food and drink only, rather than lodging. It would be better to use the word 'guesthouse' (*guesti*).

Camping

Note camping on Zanzibar is illegal and sleeping on the beach is not permitted.

Eating and drinking

Food

Cuisine on mainland Tanzania is not one of the country's main attractions. There is a legacy of uninspired British catering (soups, steaks, grilled chicken, chips, boiled vegetables, puddings, instant coffee). Tanzanians are largely big meat eaters and a standard meal is *nyama choma*, roasted beef or goat meat, usually served with a spicy relish, although some like it with a mixture of raw peppers, onions and tomato known as *kachumbari*. The main staple or starch in Tanzania is *ugali*, a mealie porridge eaten all over Africa. Small town hotels and restaurants tend to serve a limited amount of bland processed food, omelette or chicken and chips, and perhaps a meat stew but not much else. Asian eating places can be better, but are seldom of a high standard. There is a much greater variety in the cities and the tourist spots; both Dar es Salaam and Zanzibar in particular (with its exquisite coastal seafood) do a fine line in eateries. The Swahili style of cooking features aromatic curries using coconut milk, fragrant steamed rice, grilled fish and calamari, and delicious bisques made from lobster and crab. A speciality is *halau*, a sweet dessert made from almonds. Some of the larger beach resorts and safari lodges offer breakfast, lunch and dinner buffets for their all-inclusive guests, some of which can be excellent while others can be of a poor standard and there's no real way of knowing what you'll get. The most important thing is to avoid food sitting around for a long time on a buffet table, so ensure it's freshly prepared and served. Vegetarians are catered for, and fruit and vegetables are used frequently, though there is a limited choice of dishes specifically made for vegetarians on menus and you may have to make special requests. The service in Tanzanian restaurants can be somewhat slower than you are used to and it can take hours for something to materialize from a kitchen. Rather than complain just enjoy the laid-back pace and order another beer.

Various dishes can be bought at temporary roadside shelters from street vendors who prepare and cook over charcoal. It's pretty safe, despite hygiene being fairly basic, because most of the items are cooked or peeled. **Savouries** include: barbecued beef on skewers (*mishkaki*), roast maize (corn), samosas, kebabs, hard-boiled eggs and roast cassava (looks like white, peeled turnips) with red chilli-pepper garnish. **Fruits** include: oranges (peeled and halved), grapes, pineapples, bananas, mangoes (slices scored and turned inside-out), paw-paw (*papaya*) and watermelon.

Most food is bought in open air markets. In the larger towns and cities these are held daily, and as well as fresh fruit and vegetables sell eggs, bread and meat. In the smaller villages, markets are usually held on one day of the week. Markets are very colourful places to visit and as Tanzania is very fertile, just about any fruit or vegetable is available.

Drink
Local beers (lager) are decent and cheap, around US$1.40 for a 700 ml refundable bottle. Brands include Kilimanjaro and Safari lager, tasty Tusker imported from Kenya or Castle from South Africa. Imported **wines** are on the expensive side: US$10-12 in a supermarket and US$15-30 in a restaurant for a European or South African label. Tanzanian wines produced by the White Fathers at Dodoma, **Bowani Wine**, are reasonable. Wines made by the **National Milling Corporation** are undrinkable.

Spirits tend to be extremely expensive and imported brands can be found in the supermarkets and in bars. Local alternatives that are sold in both bottles and sachets of one tot include some rough vodkas and whiskies and the much more pleasant *Konyagi*, a type of scented gin, which is also produced as an alchopop, *Konyagi Ice*, with bitter lemon. Traditional Tanzanian drinks include chang'aa, a fierce spirit made from maize and sugar and then distilled. It is extremely powerful and has been known to kill so think twice before tasting any. Far more pleasant and more common is **pombe** (beer), brewed from sugar and millet or banana depending on the region. It tastes a bit like flat cider and is far more potent than it appears at first. **Palm wine** is drunk at the coast. **Soft drinks** are mainly limited to colas, orange, lemon, pineapple, ginger beer, tonic and club soda. Like beer, you have to give the bottle back when you've finished. Fresh juices are common and quite delicious. **Bottled water** is widely available and safe. **Coffee**, when fresh ground, is the local Arabica variety with a distinctive, acidic flavour. In the evenings, particularly, but all day at markets, bus and railway stations there are traditional Swahili coffee vendors with large portable conical brass coffee pots with charcoal braziers underneath. The coffee is sold black in small porcelain cups, and is excellent. They also sell peanut crisp bars and sugary cakes made from molasses. These items are very cheap and are all worth trying. On the coast chai (**tea**) is drunk in small glasses; black with lots of sugar.

Essentials A-Z

Accident and Emergency
Police, fire and ambulance T112.

Electricity
230 volts (50 cycles). The system is notorious for power surges. Computers are particularly vulnerable so take a surge protector plug (obtainable from computer stores) if you are using a laptop. New socket installations are square 3-pin but do not be surprised to encounter round 3-pin (large), round 3-pin (small) and 2-pin (small) sockets in old hotels – a multi-socket adaptor is essential. Some hotels and businesses have back-up generators in case of power cuts, which are more common at the end of the dry seasons.

Embassies and consulates
For a list of all Tanzanian embassies and consulates abroad and for all foreign embassies in Tanazania, go to www.embassygoabroad.com.

Health
The health care in the region is varied and few medical facilities are available outside the big towns. There are many excellent private and government clinics/hospitals. As with all medical care, first impressions count. If a facility is grubby then be wary of the general standard of medicine and hygiene. It's worth contacting your embassy or consulate on arrival and asking where the recommended clinics are. If you do get ill, and you have the opportunity, you should also ask your medical insurer whether they are satisfied that the medical centre or hospital that you have been referred to is of a suitable standard.

The Flying Doctors, at Wilson Airport in Nairobi covers Tanzania. A 2-week tourist membership costs US$30, 2 months US$50. It offers free evacuation by air to a medical centre or hospital. You can contact them in advance for membership and information on T+254 (0)20 315454/5, www.amref.org.

Before you go
Ideally, you should see your GP or travel clinic at least 6 weeks before your departure for general advice on travel risks, antibiotics for travellers' bacterial diarrhoea, malaria and vaccinations. Make sure you have travel insurance, The Flying Doctors based at Wilson Airport in Nairobi cover Tanzania, see above and page); get a dental check (especially if you are going to be away for more than a month); know your own blood group; and if you suffer a long-term condition such as diabetes or epilepsy make sure someone knows or that you have a Medic Alert bracelet/necklace with this information on it.

Basic vaccinations recommended include polio, tetanus, diphtheria, typhoid and hepatitis A. If you are entering the country overland, you may well be asked for a yellow fever vaccination certificate.

Diving
If you go diving make sure that you are fit do so. The **British Sub-Aqua Club (BSAC)**, Telford's Quay, South Pier Road, Ellesmere Port, Cheshire CH65 4FL, UK, T0151-350 6200, www.bsac.com, can put you in touch with doctors who do medical examinations.

Protect your feet from cuts, beach dog parasites and sea urchins. The latter are almost impossible to remove but can be dissolved with lime or vinegar. Watch for secondary infection, which you'll need antibiotics for. Serious diving injuries may require time in a decompression chamber.

Check that the dive company knows what it is doing, has appropriate certification from BSAC or **Professional Association of Diving Instructors (PADI)**, Unit 7, St Philips Central, Albert Rd, St Philips, Bristol, BS2 OTD,

T0117-300 7234, www.padi.com, and that the equipment is well maintained.

Malaria

Malaria is present in almost all of Tanzania and can cause death within 24 hrs. It can start as something just resembling an attack of flu. You may feel tired, lethargic, headachy, feverish; or, more seriously, develop fits, followed by coma and then death. Have a low index of suspicion because it is very easy to write off vague symptoms, which may actually be malaria. If you have a temperature, go to a doctor as soon as you can and ask for a malaria test. On your return home if you suffer any of these symptoms, get tested as soon as possible, even if any previous test proved negative, the test could save your life. Remember ABCD: Awareness (of whether the disease is present in the area), Bite avoidance, Chemoprophylaxis, Diagnosis.

To prevent mosquito bites wear clothes that cover arms and legs and use effective insect repellents in areas with known risks of insect-spread disease. Use a mosquito net treated with insecticide as both a physical and chemical barrier at night in the same areas. Guard against the contraction of malaria with the correct anti-malarials. Note that the Royal Homeopathic Hospital in the UK does not advocate homeopathic options for malaria prevention or treatment.

Repellents containing DEET (Di-ethyltoluamide) are the gold standard. Apply the repellent every 4-6 hrs but more often if you are sweating heavily. If a non-DEET product is used check who tested it. Validated products (tested at the London School of Hygiene and Tropical Medicine) include Mosiguard, Non-DEET Jungle formula and non-DEET Autan.

If you want to use citronella remember that it must be applied very frequently (ie hourly) to be effective. If you are a popular target for insect bites or develop lumps quite soon after being bitten, carry an Aspivenin kit.

This syringe suction device is available from many chemists and draws out some of the allergic materials and provides quick relief.

Water

There are a number of ways of purifying water. Dirty water should first be strained through a filter and then boiled or treated. Bringing water to a rolling boil at sea level is sufficient to make the water safe for drinking, but at higher altitudes you have to boil the water for a few minutes longer to ensure all microbes are killed. There are sterilizing methods that can be used and there are proprietary preparations containing chlorine or iodine compounds. Chlorine compounds generally do not kill protozoa (eg giardia). There are a number of water filters now on the market. Make sure you take the spare parts or spare chemicals with you and do not believe everything the manufacturers say.

Further information

www.bloodcare.org.uk The Blood Care Foundation (UK) will dispatch certified non-infected blood of the right type to your hospital/clinic.

www.btha.org British Travel Health Association (UK). This is the official website of an organization of travel health professionals.

www.fitfortravel.scot.nhs.uk Fit for Travel (UK). A-Z of vaccine and travel health advice requirements for each country.

www.fco.gov.uk Foreign and Common-wealth Office (FCO). This is a key travel advice site, with useful information on the country, people and climate and lists of the UK embassies/consulates.

www.masta.org Medical Advisory Service for Travellers Abroad (MASTA). A-Z of vaccine and travel health advice and requirements.

www.medicalert.co.uk Medic Alert. Produces bracelets and necklaces for those with existing medical problems, where key

medical details are engraved, so that if you collapse, a medical person can identify you.
www.travelscreening.co.uk Travel Screening Services. A private clinic that gives vaccine and travel health advice.
www.who.int World Health Organization. The WHO site has links to the WHO Blue Book on travel advice.

Books

Lankester T, *Travellers' Good Health Guide* (2nd edition, Sheldon Press, 2006).

Money

→ *US$1=TSh 1,544, £1=TSh 2,482, €1=TSh 2,169 (Jul 2011)*

Currency

The Tanzanian currency is the Tanzanian Shilling (TSh), not to be confused with the Kenyan and Uganda Shilling which are different currencies. Notes currently in circulation are TSh 200, 500, 1,000, 5,000 and 10,000. Coins are TSh 50, 10 and 20 but these are hardly worth anything and are rarely used. As it is not a hard currency, it cannot be brought into or taken out of the country, however there are no restrictions on the amount of foreign currency that can be brought into Tanzania. There are banks with ATMs and bureaux de change at both Julius Nyerere International and Zanzibar International airports. The easiest currencies to exchange are US dollars, UK pounds and euros. If you are bringing US dollars in cash, try and bring newer notes – because of the prevalence of forgery, many banks and bureaux de change do not accept US dollar bills printed before 2000. Sometimes lower denomination bills attract a lower exchange rate than higher denominations. Travellers' cheques (TCs) are widely accepted, and many hotels, travel agencies, safari companies and restaurants accept credit cards. Most banks in Tanzania are equipped to advance cash on credit cards, and increasingly most now have

ATM machines that accept Visa and Master-Card. Departure taxes can be paid in local or foreign currency, but they are usually included in the price of an air ticket.

Exchange

Visitors to Tanzania should change foreign currency at banks, bureaux de change or authorized hotels, and under no circumstances change money on the black market which is highly illegal. All banks have a foreign exchange service, and bank hours are Mon-Fri 0830-1500, Sat 0830-1330. The government has authorized bureaux de change known as forex bureaus to set rates for buying foreign currency from the public. Forex bureaux are open longer hours and offer faster service than banks and, although the exchange rates are only nominally different, the bureaus usually offer a better rate on TCs. In the large private hotels, rates are calculated directly in US$, although they can be paid in foreign or local currency. Airline fares, game park entrance fees and other odd payments to the government (such as the airport international departure tax) are also quoted in dollars, though again these can be paid for in both foreign or local currency. Just ensure that you are getting a reasonable exchange rate when the hotel or airline, etc converts US$ to TSh.

Credit cards and travellers' cheques

These are now accepted by large hotels, upmarket shops, airlines, major tour operators and travel agencies, but of course will not be taken by small hotels, restaurants and so on. There may also be a 5% fee to use them. In any town of a reasonable size you will be able to use an ATM that allow you to withdraw cash from Visa, MasterCard, Plus and Cirrus cards. Diners Club and American Express are, however, limited. Your bank will probably charge a small fee for withdrawing cash from an ATM overseas. Most banks can also organize a cash advance off your credit card. Many banks refuse to exchange travellers' cheques without being shown the purchase agreement that is, the slip issued at the point of sale that in theory you are supposed to keep separately from your travellers' cheques. Travellers' cheques are now accepted as payment for park entry fees by Tanzania National Parks, as well as cash.

Cost of travelling

In first-rate luxury lodges and tented camps expect to pay in excess of US$150 per person per night for a double rising to US$500 per night per person in the most exclusive establishments. There are half a dozen places aimed at the very top of the range tourist or honeymooner that charge nearer US$1000 per person per night. For this you will get impeccable service, cuisine and decor in fantastic locations either in the parks or on the coast. In 4- to 5-star hotels and lodges expect to spend US$200-300 a day. Careful tourists can live reasonably comfortably on US$100 a day staying in the mid-range places, though to stay in anything other than campsites on safaris, they will have to spend a little more for the cheapest accommodation in the national parks. Budget travellers can get by on US$20-30 per day using cheap guesthouses and public transport. However, with additional park entry fees and related costs, organized camping safari costs can exceed US$400 for a 3-day trip and climbing Mt Kilimanjaro is an expensive experience whatever your budget. Commodities such as chocolate and toiletries are on the expensive side, as they are imported but they are readily available. Restaurants vary widely from side-of- the-road local eateries where a simple meal of chicken and chips will cost no more than US$2-3, to the upmarket restaurants in the cities and tourists spots that can charge in excess of US$60 for 2 people with drinks.

Opening hours

Most offices will start at 0800, lunch between 1200-1300, finish business at 1700, Mon-Fri; 0900-1200 on Sat. Small shops and kiosks and markets in the bigger towns are open daily. Banks are open Mon-Fri, 0830-1530, and Sat 0830-1330. Post offices are open Mon-Fri 0800-1630, Sat 0900-1200.

Police

Calling a policeman 'sir' is customary in Tanzania. If you get in trouble with the law or have to report to the police – for any reason – *always* be exceptionally polite, even if you are reporting a crime against yourself. Tanzania police generally enjoy their authoritative status and to rant and rave and demand attention will get you absolutely nowhere.

For petty offences (driving without lights switched on, for example) police will often try to solicit a bribe, masked as an 'on-the-spot' fine. Establish the amount being requested, and then offer to go to the police station to pay, at which point you will be released with a warning. For any serious charges, immediately contact your embassy or consulate.

Safety

The majority of the people you will meet are honest and ready to help you so there is no need to get paranoid about your safety. However, theft from tourists in Tanzania does occur and it will be assumed that foreigners in the country have relative wealth. Visitors on tours or who are staying in upmarket hotels are generally very safe. Otherwise, it is sensible to take reasonable precautions by not walking around at night, and by avoiding places of known risk during the day. Petty theft and snatch robberies can be a problem, particularly in the urban areas. Don't wear jewellery or carry cameras in busy public places. Bum-bags are also very vulnerable as the belt can be cut easily. Day packs have also been known to be slashed, their entire contents drifting out on to the street without the wearer knowing. Carry money and any valuables in a slim belt under clothing.

Always lock room doors at night as noisy fans and a/c can provide cover for sneak thieves. Be wary of a driver being distracted in a parked vehicle, whilst an accomplice gets in on the other side – always keep car doors locked and windows wound up. You also need to be vigilant of thieves on public transport and guard your possessions fiercely and be wary of pickpockets in busy places like the bus and train stations. Never accept food and drink from a stranger on public transport as it might be doped so they can rob you.

Armed robberies

Unfortunately there has been a spate of armed robberies on tourists since 2007 in the Arusha area. Possibly it's the same gang. These have included an attack on a group of tourists near Lake Duluti in 2007 when 2 tourists and a tour guide were shot, and 2 armed robberies on safari vehicles near the Ngorongoro Crater in the same year. In 2008 a large group of bandits carried out 2 separate attacks on tented camps near Tarangire, and in Jan 2009 a group of tourists were robbed at gunpoint while returning to Moshi after climbing Kilimanjaro. If you are attacked at gun point, *always* give over your valuables immediately. *Never resist*. This is alarming news, but nevertheless these appear to be isolated incidents, given the amount of safari vehicles that move around the region, and hopefully the culprits will be apprehended soon.

Night driving

Crime and hazardous road conditions make travel by night dangerous. Car-jacking has occurred in both rural and urban areas. The majority of these attacks have occurred on the main road from Dar es Salaam to Zambia, between Morogoro and Mikumi National Park. Travellers are advised not to stop between populated areas, and to travel in convoys whenever possible.

Game reserves and national parks

It's not only crime that may affect your personal safety; you must also take safety precautions when visiting the game reserves and national parks. If camping, it is not advisable to leave your tent or banda during the night. Wild animals wander around the camps freely in the hours of darkness, and a protruding leg may seem like a tasty take-away to a hungry hyena. This is especially true at organized campsites, where the local animals have got so used to humans that they have lost much of their inherent fear of man. Exercise care during daylight hours too – remember wild animals can be dangerous.

Time

GMT + 3. Malawi and Zambia are GMT+2 so when crossing from Tanzania, clocks go back 1 hr.

Tipping

It is customary to tip around 10% for good service and this is greatly appreciated by hotel and restaurant staff, most of whom receive very low pay. Some of the more upmarket establishments may add a service charge to the bill. It is also expected that you tip safari guides. For information on tipping when on safari or visiting parks, see page 19.

Visas and immigration

Visas are required by all visitors except citizens of the Commonwealth (excluding citizens of the UK, Australia, New Zealand, South Africa, Canada, India and Nigeria who *do* require visas), Republic of Ireland and Iceland. Citizens of neighbouring countries do not normally require visas. For more information visit Tanzania's Ministry of Home Affairs website; www.moha.go.tz.

It is straightforward to get a visa at the point of entry (ie border crossing or airport) and many visitors find this more convenient than going to an embassy. Visas are issued at the following entry points: The road borders of Namanga, Taveta, Isebbania and Lunga Lunga (all with Kenya), Tunduma (with Zambia), Mutakula (Uganda), Rusomu (Rwanda) Songwe (Malawi, and Kilambo (Mozambique), as well as Julius Nyerere International Airport, Kilimanjaro International Airport, Zanzibar International Airport, and the ports in Zanzibar and Kigoma. Visas are paid for in US dollars, Euros or UK pounds and have been set at US$50 or e50.

Visas obtained from Tanzanian Embassies require 2 passport photographs and are issued in 24 hrs. Visitors who do not need a visa are issued with a visitor's pass on arrival, valid for 1-3 months. Your passport must be valid for a minimum of 6 months after your planned departure date from Tanzania; required whether you need a visa or not.

It is worth remembering that there is an agreement between Tanzania, Kenya and Uganda that allows holders of single entry visas to move freely between all 3 countries without the need for re-entry permits. Also remember that although part of Tanzania,

Zanzibar has its own immigration procedures and you are required to show your passport on entry and exit to the islands. You'll be stamped in and out but ensure your 3-month Tanzania doesn't expire when on Zanzibar.

Visas can be extended at the **Immigration Headquarters**, Ohio/Ghana Av, Dar es Salaam, T022-211 8637/40/43, www.moha.go.tz. Mon-Fri, 0730-1530. There are also immigration offices in Arusha and Mwanza (see pages and). You will be asked to show proof of funds (an amount of US$1000 or a credit card should be sufficient) and your return or onward airline ticket. Occasionally, independent travellers noton a tour may be asked for these at point of entry.

Resident status for people permanently employed in Tanzania visas can be arranged after arrival. Your employer will need to vouch for you, and the process can take several weeks. Because of Tanzania's 2-tiered price system for residents and non-residents, resident status does give certain privileges (lower rates on air flights, in hotels, and game park entry fees).

Weights and measures
Metric.

Contents

Footprint features

Dar es Salaam

Dar es Salaam

Dar es Salaam, meaning 'haven of peace' in Arabic, is far from peaceful these days but, by African standards at least, is a relatively relaxed, unassuming yet atmospheric city. It's hardly a hive of activity for tourists – there are a handful of local museums, art galleries and craft markets to visit, and some interesting architecture of the 'faded colonial grandeur' category alongside mosques, an attractive Lutheran church and a Roman Catholic cathedral that dominate the harbour front. But, with a rapidly increasing population estimated at 4 million, it is a thriving port, business centre and administrative base for the country (even though its status of capital city was removed in 1973), and you could do far worse than spend a couple of days here simply watching urban Tanzanian life go by. People are relaxed and friendly, the main sights of the city centre are easily walkable and it's home to some excellent international-standard hotels and restaurants.

The city dates from 1857 and was successively under the control of Zanzibar, Germany and Britain before self-determination in 1961, with all these influences leaving their mark on its character. During German occupation in the early 20th century, it was the centre of colonial administration and the main contact point between the agricultural mainland and the world of trade and commerce in the Indian Ocean and the Swahili Coast. Today, the ocean provides a sparkling backdrop to the city, with everything from small fishing boats to cruise liners and tankers visiting the port. And should the urban bustle prove too much, nearby beaches to the north and south of town provide an easy escape. Further afield, Dar is the main springboard for ferries or flights to the islands of Zanzibar, Pemba and Mafia and to game parks across the country.

Ins and outs → *Phone code: 022. Population estimated at 4,000,000. Altitude: sea level.*

Getting there

Air International and domestic flights depart from **Julius Nyerere International Airport** ① *flight information T022-284 4212, www.jnia.aero,* along Nyerere (formerly Pugu) Road, 13 km from the city centre. The airlines have desks at the airport and there are a range of facilities. For those international visitors requiring a visa for Tanzania, the visa desk is just before immigration at international arrivals. To get from the airport to the city, *dala-dala* and minibuses run regularly, are cheaper than regular taxis, but are crowded and there can be a problem with luggage, which will normally have to be accommodated on your knees. Taxis are the better option with fixed fares costing between US$25-35, depending on your destination. ▶ *For airline office details, see page 51.*

Bus The main bus station for up-country travel is on Morogoro Road in the Ubungo area, 6 km to the west of the centre. It is well organized and modern with cafés and shops and ticket offices on the main road outside. It is also reasonably secure as only ticket holders and registered taxi drivers are allowed inside; nevertheless watch out for pick pocketing. For a few shillings you can hire a porter with a trolley for luggage. A taxi into the city should cost around US$8-10. Outside on Morogoro Road, you can also catch a local bus or *dala-dala* to the centre, though again these are crowded and there is a problem if you are carrying a large amount of luggage. The best bus company recommended for foreigners, Scandinavia Express (see page 10), has an office at the Ubungo Bus Station where all their buses stop, though it also has a downtown terminal on Nyerere Road where all their services start and finish. ▶ *For details, see page 52.*

Ferry Ferries leave from the jetty on Sokoine Drive opposite St Joseph's Cathedral. Dhows and motorized boats leave from the wharf just to the south of the boat jetty, but it is now illegal for foreigners to take dhows along the coast and you would be ill-advised to arrange such a journey. The ferry companies request payment in US$ cash only and each company has a ticket office on or around the wharf. ▶ *For details, see page 52.*

Train Trains to the central regions of Tanzania (the Dar–Tabora–Kigoma/Mwanza line), run from the **Central Railway Station** ① *Sokoine Dr, T022-211 0600.* It is convenient for most hotels and is only a short walk to the ferry terminal. Trains for the southwest (the Dar–Mbeya–Zambia line) leave from **TAZARA Station** ① *T022-286 5187, www.tazara.co.tz for online reservations,* some 5 km from the centre. There are plenty of *dala-dala* and a taxi costs about US$7. ▶ *For details, see page 53.*

Getting around

Dala-dalas These are cheap at around US$0.40 for any journey (see page 11 for further information). The front of the vehicle usually has two destinations painted on the bonnet or a sign stating its destination, and sometimes another stating the fare. The main terminals in town are at the Central Railway Station (Stesheni) and the New Post Office (Posta) on Azikiwe Street. From both, if there are not enough passengers, the *dala-dala* will also make a detour to the Old Post Office on Sokoine Drive to pick up more people.

Taxis Taxis are readily available in the city centre and are parked on just about every street corner. They cost around US$2-3 per km. Any car can serve as a taxi, they are not painted in a specific colour, and they may be new or battered but serviceable. If you are visiting a non-central location and there is no taxi stand at the destination, you can always ask the driver to wait or come back and pick you up at an allotted time. These days most of Dar's taxi drivers have mobile phones, so it is easy enough to get the number and call the driver when you want to be picked up. Taxis do not have meters so always negotiate taxi fares before setting off on your journey.

Tuk-tuks (bajajis) These have increased in numbers over the past few years and are at least half the price of regular taxis. They don't go very fast, though, and are quite uncomfortable so for longer journeys stick to taxis. For more information on them, see page 12.

Tourist offices

If you contact the **Tanzania Tourist Board** ① *IPS Building, 3rd Fl, Samora Av/Azikiwe St, T022-211 1244, www.tanzaniatouristboard.com*, in advance they will post out brochures. The **Tourist Information Office** ① *Matasalamat Mansion, Samora Av, T022-213 1555, Mon-Fri 0800-1600, Sat 0830-1230*, for drop-in visitors has a limited range of glossy leaflets about the national parks and other places of interest, a noticeboard with transport timetables and fares, a (not too good) map of the city and, sometimes, a 1:2,000,000 scale map of Tanzania. Staff are very helpful, however and can also make reservations at any of the larger hotels in Tanzania and national park lodges (payment in foreign currency only) but they can't help you with budget accommodation. However, it's generally better to book the larger resort hotels and national park lodges through a travel agency or tour operator as they may offer special deals.

There are two free monthly publications available from some hotels and travel agencies; the *Dar es Salaam Guide*, which has transport timetables and good articles about destinations and sights in the city; and *What's Happening in Dar es Salaam*. The latter is better for information about upcoming events.

When to visit

The hottest months are December to the end of March, when the Indian Ocean is warm enough to swim in at night. The long rains are from March-May and the short rains November-December. The best season to visit is June-October, although there is sun all the year round, even during the rains, which are short and heavy and bring on intense humidity.

Background

Zanzibar period 1862-1886

The name Dar es Salaam means 'haven of peace' and was chosen by the founder of the city, Seyyid Majid, Sultan of Zanzibar. The harbour is sheltered, with a narrow inlet channel protecting the water from the Indian Ocean. An early British visitor in 1873, Frederic Elton, remarked that "it's healthy, the air clear – the site a beautiful one and the surrounding country green and well-wooded."

Despite the natural advantages it was not chosen as a harbour earlier, because of the difficulties of approaching through the narrow inlet during the monsoon season and

24 hours in the city

Dar es Salaam isn't brimming with life in the small hours but it is possible to spend a varied and active 24 hours here.

Start with a morning walk around the old town before it gets too hot and wander around the faded colonial architecture through to the **Botanical Gardens** and the **National Museum**. A guided walk will take you a good couple of hours. For a light lunch, call in at **L'Epi d'Or** patisserie on Samora Avenue and treat yourself to a freshly made sandwich and the best coffee in town. Then jump on a *dala-dala* to the **Makumbusho Village Museum** for a glimpse of tribal Tanzania's way of life, and take in one of their colourful dance displays in the afternoon. Make sure you spare some time for nearby **Mwenge Craft Market**, and watch expert carvers create wooden carvings and handicrafts – the best place for souvenir shopping in the city. Then head back to **Msasani Peninsula** in time for a sundowner on the terrace overlooking the bay at the **Peninsula Seaview Hotel**.

Dinner time could take you to the newest restaurant on the block – the **Oriental** at the trendy Kilimanjaro Hotel Kempinski or if you want to make the most of the seafood here, try the **Oyster Bay Grill**. **Q Bar** is the place for live music most evenings, then round off the night at **Club Bilicanos**, a world class nightclub that will keep you dancing till dawn. Just as the sun's rising, take a cab to the colourful **fish market** off Ocean Road and watch it come alive with fishermen bringing in their catch and stall-holders setting up for another busy day. Finally, wander over to the **Kigamboni** ferry port and join the locals heading south on the ferry for a brief 10-minute journey, before taking a cab a couple of kilometres to **Mikadi Beach** for a refreshing dip in the ocean or a plunge in their pool, and recover with an all-day breakfast …

there were other sites, protected by the coral reef, along the Indian Ocean coast that were used instead. However, Majid decided to construct the city in 1862 because he wanted to have a port and settlement on the mainland, which would act as a focus for trade and caravans operating to the south. Bagamoyo (see page) was already well established, but local interests there were inclined to oppose direction from Zanzibar, and the new city was a way of ensuring control from the outset.

Construction began in 1865 and the name was chosen in 1866. Streets were laid out, based around what is now Sokoine Drive running along the shoreline to the north of the inner harbour. Water was secured by the sinking of stone wells, and the largest building was the Sultan's palace. An engraving from 1869 shows the palace to have been a substantial two-storey stone building, the upper storey having sloping walls and a crenellated parapet, sited close to the shore on the present-day site of Malindi Wharf. In appearance it was similar in style to the fort that survives in Zanzibar (see page 69). To the southwest, along the shore, was a mosque and to the northwest a group of buildings, most of which were used in conjunction with trading activities. One building that survives is the double-storeyed structure now known as the Old Boma, on the corner of Morogoro Road and Sokoine Drive. The Sultan used it as an official residence for guests, and in 1867 a western-style banquet was given for the British, French, German and American consuls to launch the new city. Craftsmen and slaves were brought from Zanzibar for construction work. Coral for the masonry was cut from the reef and nearby islands. A steam tug was ordered from Germany to assist with the tricky harbour entrance and to speed up movements in the wind-sheltered inner waters. Economic life centred on agricultural cultivation (particularly coconut plantations) and traders who dealt with the local Zaramo people as well as with the long-distance caravan traffic.

Dar es Salaam suffered its first stroke of ill-luck when Majid died suddenly in 1870, after a fall in his new palace, and he was succeeded as Sultan by his half-brother, Seyyid Barghash. Barghash did not share Majid's enthusiasm for the new settlement, and indeed Majid's death was taken to indicate that carrying on with the project would bring ill-fortune. The court remained in Zanzibar. Bagamoyo and Kilwa predominated as mainland trading centres. The palace and other buildings were abandoned, and the fabric rapidly fell into decay. Nevertheless the foundation of a Zaramo settlement and Indian commercial involvement had been established.

Despite the neglect, Barghash maintained control over Dar es Salaam through an agent (*akida*) and later a governor (*wali*) and Arab and Baluchi troops. An Indian customs officer collected duties for use of the harbour and the Sultan's coconut plantations were maintained. Some commercial momentum had been established, and the Zaramo traded gum copal (a residue used in making varnishes), rubber, coconuts, rice and fish for cloth, ironware and beads. The population expanded to around 5000 by 1887, and comprised a cosmopolitan mixture of the Sultan's officials, soldiers, planters, traders, and shipowners, as well as Arabs, Swahilis and Zaramos, Indian Muslims, Hindus and a handful of Europeans.

German period 1887-1916

In 1887 the German East African Company under Hauptmann Leue took up residence in Dar es Salaam. They occupied the residence of the Sultan's governor whom they succeeded in getting recalled to Zanzibar, took over the collection of customs dues and, in return for a payment to the Zaramo, obtained a concession on the land. The Zaramo, Swahili and Arabs opposed this European takeover, culminating in the Arab revolt of 1888-1889, which involved most of the coastal region as well as Dar es Salaam. The city came under sporadic attack and the buildings of the Berlin Mission, a Lutheran denomination located on a site close to the present Kivukoni ferry, were destroyed. When the revolt was crushed, and the German government took over responsibility from the German East Africa Company in 1891, Dar es Salaam was selected as the main centre for administration and commercial activities.

The Germans laid out a grid street system, built the railway to Morogoro, connected the town to South Africa by overland telegraph, and laid underwater electricity cables to Zanzibar. Development in Dar es Salaam involved the construction of many substantial buildings, and most of these survive today. In the quarter of a century to 1916, several fine buildings were laid out on Wilhelms Ufer (now Kivukoni Front), and these included administrative offices as well as a club and a casino. Landing steps to warehouses, and a hospital, were constructed on the site of the present Malindi Wharf and behind them the railway station. Just to the south of Kurasini Creek was the dockyard where the present deep-water docks are situated. A second hospital was built at the eastern end of Unter den Akazien and Becker Strasse, now Samora Avenue. The post office is on what is now Sokoine Drive at the junction with Mkwepu Street. A governor's residence provided the basis for the current State House. The principal hotels were the Kaiserhof, which was demolished to build the New Africa Hotel, and the Burger Hotel, razed to make way for the present Telecoms building. The area behind the north harbour shore was laid out with fine acacia-lined streets and residential two-storey buildings with pitched corrugated-iron roofs and first-floor verandas, and most of these survive. Behind the east waterfront were shops and office buildings, many of which are still standing.

British period 1916-1961

In the 45 years that the British administered Tanganyika, public construction was kept to a minimum on economy grounds, and business was carried on in the old German buildings. The governor's residence was damaged by naval gunfire in 1915, and was remodelled to form the present State House. In the 1920s, the Gymkhana Club was laid out on its present site behind Ocean Road, and Mnazi Moja ('Coconut Grove') established as a park. The Selander Bridge causeway was constructed, and this opened up the Oyster Bay area to residential construction for the European community. The Yacht Club was built on the harbour shore (it is now the customs post) and behind it the Dar es Salaam Club (now the Hotel and Tourism Training Centre), both close to the Kilimanjaro Hotel Kempinski.

As was to be expected, road names were changed, as well as those of the most prominent buildings. Thus Wilhelms Ufer became Azania Front, Unter den Akazien became Acacia Avenue, Kaiser Strasse became City Drive. Other streets were named after explorers Speke and Burton, and there was a Windsor Street. One departure from the relentless Anglicization of the city was the change of Bismarck Strasse to Versailles Street – it was the Treaty of Versailles in 1918 that allocated the former German East Africa to the British.

The settling by the various groups living in the city into distinctive areas was consolidated during the British period. Europeans lived in Oyster Bay to the north of the city centre, in large Mediterranean-style houses with arches, verandas and gardens surrounded by solid security walls and fences. The Asians lived either in tenement-style blocks in the city centre or in the Upanga area in between the city and Oyster Bay, where they built houses and bungalows with small gardens. African families built Swahili-style houses, initially in the Kariakoo area to the west of the city. Others were accommodated in government bachelor quarters provided for railway, post office and other government employees. As population increased, settlement spread out to Mikocheni and along Morogoro Road and to Mteni to the south.

Independence 1961-present

For the early years of independence Dar es Salaam managed to sustain its enviable reputation of being a gloriously located city with a fine harbour, generous parklands with tree-lined avenues (particularly in the Botanical Gardens and Gymkhana area), and a tidy central area of shops and services. New developments saw the construction of high-rise government buildings, most notably the Telecoms building on the present Samora Avenue, the New Africa Hotel, the massive cream and brown Standard Bank Building (now National Bank of Commerce) on the corner of Sokoine Drive and Maktaba Street, and the Kilimanjaro Hotel on a site next to the Dar es Salaam Club on Kivukoni Front.

But with the Arusha Declaration of 1967, many buildings were nationalized and somewhat haphazardly occupied. The new tenants of the houses, shops and commercial buildings were thus inclined to undertake minimal repairs and maintenance. In many cases it was unclear who actually owned the buildings. The city went into steady decline, and it is a testament to the sturdy construction of the buildings from the German period that so many of them survive. Roads fell into disrepair and the harbour became littered with rusting hulks.

The new government changed the names of streets and buildings, to reflect a change away from the colonial period. Thus Acacia became Independence Avenue, the Prince of Wales Hotel became the Splendid. Later names were chosen to pay tribute to African leaders – Independence Avenue changed to Samora, and Pugu Road became Nkrumah Street. President Nyerere decided that no streets or public buildings could be named after living Tanzanians, and so it was only after his death that City Drive was named after Prime Minister Edward Sokoine.

Old Dar es Salaam was saved by two factors. First, the economic decline that began in the 1970s meant that there were limited resources for building new modern blocks for which some of old colonial buildings would have had to make way. Second, the government decided in 1973 to move the capital to Dodoma. This didn't stop new government construction entirely, but it undoubtedly saved many historic buildings.

In the early 1980s, Dar es Salaam reached a low point, not dissimilar from the one reached almost exactly a century earlier with the death of Sultan Majid. In 1992 things began to improve. Colonial buildings have now been classified as of historical interest and are to be preserved. Japanese aid has allowed a comprehensive restoration of the road system. Several historic buildings, most notably the Old Boma on Sokoine Drive, the Ministry of Health building on Luthuli Road and the British Council headquarters on Samora Avenue, have been restored or are undergoing restoration. Civic pride is returning. The Askari Monument has been cleaned up and the flower beds replanted, the Cenotaph Plaza relaid, pavements and walkways repaired and the Botanical Gardens restored. Very usefully, new signposts are a feature throughout the city, which not only clearly show the street names but places of interest, hotels, and major institutions such as banks or embassies. The main road into Dar es Salaam – the 109 km branch road off the Arusha– Mbeya road that neatly dissects the middle of the country – was for years a ribbon of potholed and broken tar. But this too has been upgraded into super-smooth highway thanks to foreign aid.

Sights

The best way to discover the heart of Dar es Salaam is on foot and we have suggested two half-day walks that take in most of the historic buildings. An alternative is to join a guided **walking tour** ① *2½ hr morning walks through the old town cost around US$35 adult, US$15 child depending on the tour operator, with discounts for groups, and including tastings of Swahili, Arab and Indian foods.* Ask the tourist office to recommend a tour operator.

Walking tour of the old town

A walking tour (about half a day) of the historic parts of old Dar es Salaam might start at the **Askari Monument** at the junction of Samora Avenue and Azikwe Street. Originally on this site was a statue to Major Hermann von Wissmann, the German explorer and soldier, who suppressed the coastal Arab Revolt of 1888-1889 and went on to become governor of German East Africa in 1895-1896. This first statue erected in 1911 depicted a pith-helmeted Wissmann, one hand on hip, the other on his sword, gazing out over the harbour with an African soldier at the base of the plinth draping a German flag over a reclining lion. It was demolished in 1916 when the British occupied Dar es Salaam, as were statues to Bismarck and Carl Peters. The present bronze statue, in memory of all those who died in the First World War, but principally dedicated to the African troops and porters, was unveiled in 1927. The statue was cast by Morris Bronze Founders of Westminster, London, and the sculptor was James Alexander Stevenson (1881-1937), who signed himself 'Myrander'. There are two bronze bas-reliefs on the sides of the plinth by the same sculptor, and the inscription, in English and Swahili, is from Rudyard Kipling.

Proceeding towards the harbour, on the left is the **New Africa Hotel** on the site where the old **Kaiserhof Hotel** stood. This was once the finest building in Dar es Salaam, the venue for the expat community to meet for sundowners. The terrace outside overlooked the Lutheran church and the harbour, while a band played in the inner courtyard. Across Sokoine Drive, on the left is the **Lutheran cathedral** with its distinctive red-tiled spire and tiled canopies over the windows to provide shade. Construction began in 1898. Opposite is the **Cenotaph**, again commemorating the 1914-1918 war, which was unveiled in 1927 and restored in 1992.

Turning left along Kivukoni Front, there is a fine view through the palm trees across the harbour. Just past Ohio Street, on the shore side, is the **Old Yacht Club**. Prior to the removal of the club to its present site on the west side of Msasani Peninsula in 1967, small boats bobbing at anchor in the bay were a feature of the harbour. The Old Yacht Club buildings now house the harbour police headquarters.

Opposite the Old Yacht Club is the site of the German Club for civilians, which was expanded to form the Dar es Salaam (DSM) Club in the British period. It used to have a spacious terrace and a handsome bar. On the first floor are rooms that were used for accommodation, with verandas facing inward and outside stone staircases. Evelyn Waugh once stayed here. Today, after substantial renovation, this building is the smart new **Kilimanjaro Hotel Kempinski**, one of Dar's most luxurious hotels.

Further along Kivukoni Front is the first of an impressive series of German government buildings. The first two, one now the High Court, and the other the present Magistrates' Court on the corner of Luthuli Road, were for senior officials. In between is the old **Secretariat**, which housed the governor's offices. On the other corner of Luthuli Road is the German Officers' Mess, where some gambling evidently took place as it became known as the **Casino**. These buildings are exceptional, and it is a tribute to the high quality construction of the German period that they have survived, with virtually no maintenance for the past 30 years. Construction was completed in 1893. On the high ground further along Kivukoni Front is the site of the first European building in Dar, the **Berlin Mission**. It was built in 1887, extensively damaged in the 1888-1889 uprising and demolished in 1959 to make way for a hotel, which, in the event, was not constructed.

The eastern part of the city resembles an eagle's head (it is said the Msasani Peninsula is one of the eagle's wings). At the tip of the eagle's beak was a pier, just where the fish market (see page 34) stands today, constructed in the British period for the use of the governor. This was just a little further round the promontory from the present ramp for the ferry that goes over to Kigamboni. Past Magogoni Street is the **Swimming Club** (see page 50), constructed in the British period and now mostly used by the Asian community.

Following Ocean Road, on the left is the present **State House**, with a drive coming down to gates. This was the original German governor's residence. It had tall, Islamic-style arches on the ground floor rather similar to those in the building today, but the upper storey was a veranda with a parapet and the roof was supported on cast-iron columns. The building was bombarded by British warships in 1914 and extensively damaged. In 1922 it was rebuilt and the present scalloped upper-storey arches added, as well as the tower with the crenellated parapet.

The **German Hospital** is further along Ocean Road with its distinctive domed towers topped by a clusters of iron spikes. It is an uneasy mixture of the grand (the towers) and the utilitarian (the corrugated-iron roofing). It was completed in 1897 and was added to

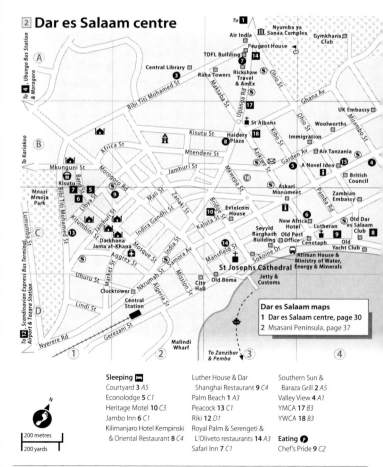

② Dar es Salaam centre

Sleeping 🛏

Courtyard **3** A5
Econolodge **5** C1
Heritage Motel **10** C3
Jambo Inn **6** C1
Kilimanjaro Hotel Kempinski
& Oriental Restaurant **8** C4

Luther House & Dar
Shanghai Restaurant **9** C4
Palm Beach **1** A3
Peacock **13** C1
Riki **12** D1
Royal Palm & Serengeti &
L'Oliveto restaurants **14** A3

Southern Sun &
Baraza Grill **2** A5
Valley View **4** A1
YMCA **17** B3
YWCA **18** B3

Eating 🍴

Chef's Pride **9** C2

Dar es Salaam maps
1 Dar es Salaam centre, page 30
2 Msasani Peninsula, page 37

200 metres
200 yards

during the British period with single-storey, bungalow-style wards to the rear.

Turning left past the baobab tree down Chimera Road and taking the left fork, Luthuli Road leads to the junction with Samora Avenue. Here stood the statue of Bismarck, a replica of the celebrated Regas bust. The area either side of this boulevard, one of the glories of Dar es Salaam in the German era, was laid out as an extensive park. The flamboyant trees and *oreodoxa* (Royal Palms) still border it.

The first Director of Agriculture, Professor Stuhlmann, began laying out the **Botanical Gardens** in 1893. The building that houses the Agriculture Department as well as the Meteorological Station and the Government Geographer lies just to the southwest and was completed in 1903, by which time the gardens were well established, Stuhlmann using his position as Chief Secretary from 1900-1903 to channel resources to their development. The gardens became the home of the Dar es Salaam Horticultural Society, which still has a building on the site, and has undergone some rehabilitation with most of the exhibits labelled. Now, though, it's in need of some further care and attention, although it's a welcome escape from the city and the peacocks give it an air of exoticism. It is one of the few places in the world to see the coco-de-mer palm tree apart from the Seychelles.

To the left of the gardens is **Karimjee Hall**, built by the British and which served as the home of the Legislative Council prior to independence. It then became the home of the National Assembly, the Bunge. In the same area is the original **National Museum** (see page 33), a single-storey stone building with a red-tiled roof and arched windows constructed as the King George V Memorial Museum in 1940, changing its name in 1963. A larger, modern building was constructed later to house exhibits, and the old building was used as offices.

Turning left down Shaaban Robert Street, on the other side of Sokoine Drive, in a crescent behind the Speaker's Office is the first school built in Dar es Salaam (1899) by the German government. It was predominantly for Africans, but also had a few Indian pupils, all children of state-employed officials (*akidas*). Walking west down Sokoine Drive you return to the New Africa Hotel.

Chinese **4** *B4*
City Garden **5** *B4*
Cynics' Café & Wine Bar **7** *A3*
Debonair's & Steer's **15** *B4*
Garden Food Court at
  Haidery Plaza **8** *B3*
Sawasdee **6** *C4*
Sichaun **3** *A2*

Sno-cream **14** *C3*

Bars & clubs 🌀
Club Bilicanas **16** *B3*

Walking tour of the City

A second half-day walking tour might begin at the **New Africa Hotel** and proceed west along Sokoine Street past the National Bank of Commerce building on the right. On the corner with Mkwepa Street is the German **Post Office** completed in 1893. Although the façade has been remodelled to give it a more modern appearance, the structure is basically unchanged. Just inside the entrance is a plaque to the memory of members of the Signals Corps who lost their lives in the First World War in East Africa. There are some 200 names listed with particularly heavy representation from South Africa and India whose loyalty to the British Empire drew them into the conflict.

On the opposite corner to the post office is the site of the old customs headquarters, the **Seyyid Barghash Building**, constructed around 1869. The building on the corner with Bridge Street is the modern multi-storey **Wizaraya Maji, Nishati na Madim** (Ministry of Water, Energy and Minerals), which is on the site of the old Customs House. Next door, sandwiched between the ministry building and Forodhani Secondary School, is the **White Fathers' House** – called **Atiman House**. It is named after a heroic and dedicated doctor, Adrian Atiman, who was redeemed from slavery in Niger by White Father missionaries, educated in North Africa and Europe, and who worked for decades as a doctor in Tanzania until his death, circa 1924. Atiman House was constructed in the 1860s in the Zanzibar period and is the oldest surviving house in the city, excluding administrative buildings. It was built as a residence for the Sultan of Zanzibar's Dar es Salaam wives, and sold by the Sultan to the White Fathers in 1922. In the visitors' parlour are two extremely interesting old photographs of the waterfront at Dar es Salaam as it was in German colonial times.

Continuing along Sokoine Drive to the west, the next building is **St Joseph's Roman Catholic Cathedral**. Construction began in 1897 and took five years to complete. St Joseph's remains one of the most striking buildings in Dar es Salaam, dominating the harbour front. It has an impressive vaulted interior, shingle spire and a fine arrangement of arches and gables. Next to the cathedral was Akida's Court.

On the corner of Morogoro Road is Dar's oldest surviving building, the **Old Boma** dating from 1867. It was built to accommodate the visitors of Sultan Majid and features a fine Zanzibar door and coral-rag walls. On the opposite corner is the **City Hall**, a very handsome building with an impressive façade and elaborate decoration.

On the corner of Uhuru Street is the **Railway Station**, a double-storey building with arches and a pitched-tile roof, the construction of which began in 1897. Between the station and the shore was the site of the palace of Sultan Majid and of the hospital for Africans constructed in 1895 by Sewa Haji, but which was demolished in 1959.

Turning right in front of the railway station leads to the **clock tower**, a post-war concrete construction erected to celebrate the elevation of Dar es Salaam to city status in 1961. A right turn at the clock tower leads along Samora Avenue and back to the Askari Monument.

There are other notable buildings in the City. On Mosque Street is the ornate **Darkhana Jama'at-Khana** of the Ismaili community, three storeys high with a six-storey tower on the corner topped by a clock, a pitched roof and a weathervane.

There are several other mosques, two (**Ibaddhi Mosque** and **Memon Mosque**) on Mosque Street itself (clearly signposted and stringed with coloured lights used for religious occasions), one on Kitumbini Street, one block to the southwest of Mosque Street, (a **Sunni mosque** with an impressive dome), and there are two mosques on Bibi

Titi Mohamed Street, the **Ahmadiyya mosque** near the junction with Pugu Road and the other close by. On Kitsu Street, there are two Hindu temples, and on Upanga Road is a grand Ismaili building decorated with coloured lights during festivals.

St Alban's Church on the corner of Upanga Road and Maktaba Street was constructed in the interwar period. St Alban's is a grand building modelled on the Anglican church in Zanzibar. This is the Anglican Church of the Province of Tanzania, and was the Governor's church in colonial times. The **Greek Orthodox church**, further along Upanga Street, was constructed in the 1940s. **St Peter's Catholic Church**, off the Bagamoyo Road, was constructed in 1962, and is in modern style with delicate concrete columns and arches.

The Museum and House of Culture Dar es Salaam (formerly National Museum)

ⓘ *Shaaban Robert St next to the Botanical Gardens, between Sokoine Dr and Samora Av, T022-211 7508, www.houseofculture.or.tz. Daily 0930-1800. Entry US$5. Student US$2.*

The Museum opened in 1940 in the former King George V Memorial Museum building next to the Botanical Gardens. King George V's car can still be seen in the newer wing, which was built in front of the old museum in 1963. The museum is in a garden where a few peacocks stroll and where there is a sculpture in memory of victims of the 1989 American Embassy bombing. Created in 2004 by US artist Elyn Zimmerman, it comprises a group of six related geometric forms that surround a granite-rimmed pool. Their flatness and thinness, as well as their striking silhouettes and outlines, were inspired by shapes used in traditional African art, shields and other objects including Tanzanian stools, which Zimmerman said greatly influenced her work. Very interestingly, the very same artist designed the World Trade Centre Memorial in 1993, after a bomb set by terrorists exploded on the site of the World Trade Centre in New York. That sculpture was a cenotaph to an attack that predated both the 7 August 1998 bombings in Dar es Salaam and Nairobi, and the 11 September 2001 attacks in New York. Zimmerman's 1993 sculpture was destroyed in the 2001 attack at the World Trade centre.

The museum has excellent ethnographic, historical and archaeological collections. The old photographs are particularly interesting. Traditional craft items, headdresses, ornaments, musical instruments and witchcraft accoutrements are on display. Artefacts representing Tanzanian history date from the slave trade to the post-colonial period. Fossils from Olduvai Gorge kept there include those of Zinjanthropus – sometimes referred to as Zinj or 'nutcracker man' – the first of a new group of hominid remains collectively known as *Australopithecus boisei*, discovered by Mary Leakey. The coastal history is represented by glazed Chinese porcelain pottery and a range of copper coins from Kilwa. One of the more unusual exhibits is a bicycle in working order made entirely of wood. The museum also regularly stages exhibitions – see press for details.

West towards Kariakoo

The area to the northwest of India Street, on either side of Morogoro Road, was an Asian section of the city in the colonial period, and to a large extent still is. Buildings are typically several storeys high, the ground floor being given over to business with the upper storeys being used for residential accommodation. The façades are often ornate, with the name of the proprietor and the date of construction prominently displayed. Two superb examples on Morogoro Road, near Africa Street, are the premises of M Jessa. One was a cigarette and tobacco factory and the other a rice mill.

Casuarina cones

A particularly fine set of casuarina trees can be found along Ocean Road in Dar es Salaam. Strangely, they are also found in Australia. Quite unlike most other trees in East Africa, the theory is that the seed-bearing cones were carried by the cold tidal currents from the west coast of Australia into the equatorial waters flowing west across the Indian Ocean to the shore of Tanzania and then north along the East African coast in the Somalia current, eventually germinating after a journey of about 10,000 km.

Further to the west is the open Mnazi Mmoja (coconut grove) with the **Uhuru Monument** dedicated to the freedom that came with independence, and celebrations take place here every year on 9 December to commemorate Independence Day. The original Uhuru monument is a white obelisk with a flame – the Freedom Torch. A second concrete monument, designed by R Ashdown, was erected to commemorate 10 years of independence. This was enlivened with panels by a local artist. On the far side of the space is **Kariakoo**, laid out in a grid pattern and predominantly an African area. It became known as Kariakoo during the latter part of the First World War when African porters (the carrier corps, from which the current name is derived) were billeted here after the British took over the city in 1916. The houses are Swahili style. The colourful **market** in the centre and the shark market on the junction of Msimbazi and Tandamuti streets are well worth a visit but watch out for pickpockets.

Fish market and Banda Beach

At the point of the eagle's beak, where the ferry leaves for Kigamboni, is the **Integrated Fish Market Complex**. A fish market has been on this site since time immemorial, formerly part of an old fishing village called Mzizima, which was located between what is now State House and Ocean Road Hospital. The village met its demise when Seyyid Majid founded Dar es Salaam in 1862, although the fish market survived. In 2002, the Japanese government funded a substantial expansion programme and a new fish market was built. There are now zones for fish cleaning, fish frying, one for shellfish and vegetables, another for firewood and charcoal, an auction hall for wholesale vendors and buyers, and a maintenance area for the repair of boats, fishing nets and other tools of the trade. The complex is one of a kind and provides employment for 100 fishermen catering to thousands of daily shoppers. As you can imagine, this is an extremely smelly place. Fresh fish can be bought here and there is an astonishingly wide variety of seafood from blue fish, lobster, red snapper, to calamari and prawns. Be warned though, the vendors are quite aggressive and you'll need to haggle hard. You can also buy ice here to pack the fish.

Just north of the market is a stretch of sand known as **Banda Beach**, a well-known place for sittin' on the dock of the bay. Fishing boats, mostly lateen-sailed *ngalawas*, are beached on the shore.

Gymkhana Club

Further along Ocean Road, past State House and the hospital, are the grounds of the Gymkhana Club, which extend down to the shore. Amongst other sports practised here (see page 49) is golf, and there is an 18-hole course featuring what are called 'browns' as opposed to 'greens'. There were various cemeteries on the shore side of the golf course, a European cemetery between the hospital and Ghana Avenue, and a Hindu crematorium beyond.

Nyumba ya Sanaa Complex

ⓘ *Junction of Ohio St, Ali Mwinyi Rd and Bibi Titi Mohammed St, northwest of the Royal Palm Hotel, T022-213 1727. Open Mon-Fri 0800-2000, Sat-Sun 0800-1600.*

This art gallery has displays of paintings in various styles including oil, watercolour and chalk, as well as carvings and batiks. You can see the artists at work, and there is also a café on site. The centre was started by a nun and the present building was constructed with help from a Norwegian donation in the early 1980s. Traditional dances are held here on Friday evenings at 1930.

Oyster Bay

At the intersection of Ocean Road and Ufukoni Road on the shore side is a rocky promontory which was the site of European residential dwellings constructed in the interwar period by the British. These are either side of Labon Drive (previously Seaview Road). Continuing along Ocean Road is Selander Bridge, a causeway over the Msimbazi Creek, a small river edged by marsh that circles back to the south behind the main part of the city. Beyond Selander Bridge, on the ocean side, is Oyster Bay, which became the main European residential area in the colonial era (Rita Hayworth had a house here), and today is the location of many diplomatic missions. There are many spacious dwellings, particularly along Kenyatta Drive, which looks across the bay. The area in front of the recently refurbished **Oysterbay Hotel** is a favourite place for parking and socializing in the evenings and at weekends, particularly by the Asian community. Ice cream sellers and barbecue kiosks have sprung up on the shore in the last few years.

Around Dar

Makumbusho Village Museum

ⓘ *Bagamoyo Rd, about 9 km from the city centre, on the right-hand side of the road just before the Peacock Hotel Millennium Towers, T022-270 0437, www.villagemuseum.home stead.com. Open daily 0930-1900, US$3, Tanzanians and children US$1, photos US$3, video cameras US$20. Taxis cost about US$10 from the city centre, or dala-dala from the New Post Office (Posta) heading towards Mwenge, which pass the entrance. Ask for Makumbusho bus stop or get off when you see the tall Millennium Towers Hotel and walk back a few metres.*

The museum gives a compact view of the main traditional dwelling styles of Tanzania, with examples of artists and craftsmen at work. There are constructions of tribal homesteads from 18 ethnic groups with examples of furnished dwelling huts, cattle pens, meeting huts and, in one case, an iron-smelting kiln. Traditional dances are performed daily from 1400 to 1800 with performers recruited from all over Tanzania. It's worthwhile having a guide to explain the origin of the dances, which end with a display of tumbling and acrobatics. There is a café, and an unusual compound, the Makumbusho Social Club, where the public is welcome. The small, corrugated-iron, partly open-sided huts are each named after one of Tanzania's game parks.

Kigamboni

The beaches on Kigamboni are the best close to the city and, like on the beaches to the north, the resorts here (see Sleeping page 42) are popular with day visitors especially at the weekends. The Kigamboni ferry (which takes cars) leaves from the harbour mouth close to the fish market, just before Kivukoni Front becomes Ocean Road, at regular intervals during the day. The ferry runs from 0600 to midnight and costs US$1 per vehicle and US$0.25 per person. Foot passengers can walk directly on to the ferry from the city side and at Kigamboni catch taxis and *dala-dala* that follow the beach road for several kilometres to where most of the more accessible resorts are. Hotels such as **Ras Kutani** and the **Amani Beach Hotel** are further down this road, around 30 km from the ferry, and you will need to contact these lodges to arrange transport if you are not driving yourself.

The small town of Kigamboni spreads up from where the ferry docks and is the site of Kivukoni College, which provided training for CCM party members, but has now been turned into a school and a social science academy. Just before the college, which faces across the harbour to Kivukoni Front, is the Anglican church and a free- standing bell. The Anglican church was formerly a Lutheran church. The new Lutheran church, a fine modern building, lies 500 m into Kigamboni. On the Indian Ocean shore side there are several small enterprises making lime by burning cairns of coral.

Gezaulole

① *Part of the Cultural Tourism Programme operated from Arusha. Further details available at Tanzanian tourist information centre in Arusha, T027-2503 8403, www.infojep.com/culturaltours. Brochures for each project can be downloaded from the website.*
The coastal village of Gezaulole lies 13 km or half an hour's drive southeast of the ferry at Kigamboni, reachable by *dala-dala*. This was chosen as one of the first Ujamaa villages, part of an ultimately unsuccessful settlement policy of the early 1970s, in which people from many areas of the country were relocated to form agricultural communes. In earlier days it was a Zaramo settlement and they gave the village the name Gezaulole, which means 'Try and See' in the Kizaramo language. Today, the community has an active role in a cultural tourism programme that offers walks through the village and on the beach, short trips on a local dhow and visits to an old slave depot and a 400- year-old mosque. It is possible to stay with a local family, though it is easy enough to reach on a day trip. Inexpensive and tasty local meals are available and can be eaten with one of the families even if you are not staying for the night. Locally made handicrafts are also for sale. Profits from the programme go towards buying equipment for the local school.

Northern beaches

① *To get to either beach, a taxi from the city will cost in the region of US$15. To get to Kunduchi by public transport take a* dala-dala *from the New Post Office (Posta) in the city to Mwenge about 10 km along the Bagomoyo Rd, then change to one heading to Kunduchi (clearly signposted on the bonnet of the vehicle). Both rides will cost US$0.30. To get to Mbezi, take the same Kunduchi* dala-dala *from Mwenge, and at the sign for the White Sands Hotel on Bagomoyo Rd a couple of kilometres before the Kunduchi turn off, ask to get off (look out for the Kobil service station). At this junction you can catch a bicycle taxi for US$0.70 or a tuk-tuk for US$2, the couple of kilometres to the hotels. Do not walk along this road, as there have been muggings.*

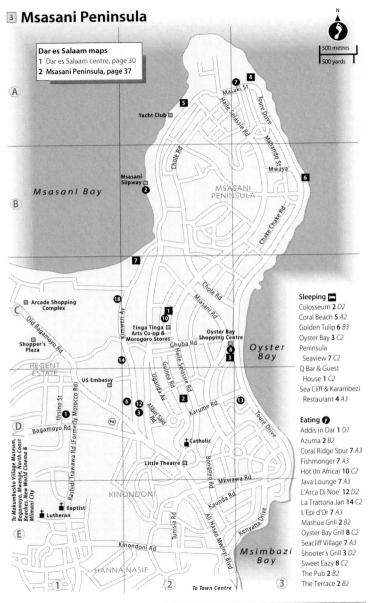

3 Msasani Peninsula

N

500 metres
500 yards

Dar es Salaam maps
1 Dar es Salaam centre, page 30
2 Msasani Peninsula, page 37

Masaki St

Yacht Club

Haile Selassie Rd

Toure Drive

Mahando St

Chole Rd

Msasani Slipway

Mwaya

MSASANI PENINSULA

Msasani Bay

Chake Chake Rd

Chole Rd

Masani Rd

Arcade Shopping Complex

Old Bagamoyo Rd

Kimweri Av

Shopper's Plaza

Tinga Tinga Arts Co-op & Morogoro Stores

Oyster Bay Shopping Centre

Ghuba Rd

Oyster Bay

REGENT ESTATE

US Embassy

Haile Selassie Rd

Guinea Rd

Uganda Av

Albin Sjad Rd

Karume Rd

Ursino St

Bagamoyo Rd

Rashidi Trawawa Rd (Formerly Morocco Rd)

Pol

† Catholic

Little Theatre

Bongoyo Rd

Mkwawa Rd

Toure Drive

To Makumbusho Village Museum, Bagamoyo, Mwenge, North Coast Beaches, New World Cinema & Mlimani City

KINONDONI

Kaunda Rd

Ali Hasan Mwinyi Blvd

Kenyata Drive

Baptist

Lutheran

Kinondoni Rd

HANNA NASIF

Pd Isingu

Msimbazi Bay

2

To Town Centre

3

The shore close to Dar es Salaam is not particularly good for swimming. The best beaches are at **Kunduchi**, some 25 km north of the city, and **Mbezi Beach,** 20 km north of the city. These beaches are separated by a lagoon but both are accessed along side roads off the Bagamoyo Road and are easily reached by good tarmac roads. Most of the hotels and resorts along this coast (see page 43) welcome day visitors who want to enjoy the facilities and beaches, including **Silver Sands Hotel, Kunduchi Beach Hotel, Bahari Beach Hotel, Jangwani Sea Breeze Resort** and the **White Sands Hotel.** Some charge a fee of US$5-10 for the day, and it's worth paying to use the hotels' private (and guarded) beaches – the stretches of beach between the hotels should not be visited unaccompanied, people have been mugged here. Some also charge an extra fee if you bring your own food and drink. This is because many Indian families bring full-on picnics for a day at the beach and the hotel benefits little from selling food and drink. Most have restaurants and bars with bands playing at weekends and public holidays, and some offer a variety of excursions to nearby islands and also windsurfing. Snorkelling is a bit hit and miss because the water is not always very clear, especially during the rainy seasons.

There is a good beach on the uninhabited **Bongoyo Island**, 2 km north of Msasani Peninsula. The island is a marine reserve popular for diving and snorkelling, and there are a few short walking trails, good beaches and simple seafood meals are available. A popular destination for a day trip from Dar es Salaam, boats take 30 minutes, cost US$14 return and leave from **The Slipway** on Msasani Peninsula at 0930,1130, 1330 and 1530, returning approximately one hour later. A similarly good beach can be found on **Mbudya Island**, 4 km north of Bongoyo Island, but there are no facilities here. Boat rides are available from **White Sands Hotel, Jangwani Sea Breeze Resort** and **Bahari Beach Hotel.**

Diving
On the mainland, local divers recommend the offshore islands around Dar es Salaam, though mainland reefs accessible from Tanga and Dar have been damaged through the illegal practice of dynamite fishing, which, through slack policing, is still a problem today. However, if you are not visiting Pemba or Zanzibar and need to get wet, there are a number of memorable dive sites around Dar worth a dip or two. Of particular note is Ferns Wall, which is on the seaward side of Fungu Yasin Reef, where you'll find large barrel sponges, gorgonian fans and 2-m long whip corals. Reef sharks are often spotted here. Because of its depth this site is for advanced divers only. Another favourite is Mwamba, a unique reef comprising large fields of pristine brain, rose and plate corals. Although slightly further out, Big T reef is a must dive for the experienced diver but only on a calm day. Latham Island, southwest of Dar, is an area surrounded by deep water where big game fish and elusive schools of hammerheads can be found. It can only be dived with a very experienced skipper who knows the area. ▸▸ *For further details, see Activities and tours, page 49.*

Kisarawe and Pugu Hills Forest Reserve
ⓘ *Follow the airport road to the south of the city. Buses to Kisarawe leave from Narungumbe St (next to the Tanzania Postal Bank on Msimbazi St in Kariakoo) about once an hour and cost US$2. To get to Pugu, turn left at the Agip petrol station in Kisarawe and the track into the reserve is a little further along on the right. It's 3 km from Kisarawe and if you're driving you'll need a 4WD.*

In the peaceful rural hill town of Kisarawe it is hard to believe that you are just 32 km southwest from the hustle and bustle of Dar es Salaam. During the colonial period Kisarawe was used by European residents of the capital as a kind of hill station to escape from the coastal heat. It receives a higher rainfall than Dar because of its slightly increased elevation. There is little to see in the town itself but the surrounding countryside is very attractive, in particular the nearby rainforest at Pugu Hills Forest Reserve about 3-4 km from the centre of Kisarawe town. It constitutes one of the few remaining parts of a coastal forest, which 10 million years ago extended from Mozambique to northern Kenya. It was gazetted as a reserve in 1954, at which time it stretched all the way to Dar's international airport and was home to many big game animals, including lions, hippos and elephants. Since then the natural growth of the metropolis, as well as the urban demand for charcoal (coupled with the lack of alternative sources of income), has seen a large reduction in the forested area. In the past few years a concerted effort has been made to counter this process and a nature trail has been established in order to encourage people to visit the area. Although Pugu contains flora and fauna which are unique to the forests of this district, you are unlikely to come across many animals in the forest; but it is a very beautiful spot and the perfect tonic for those in need of a break from Dar es Salaam. Most visitors spend the night in the new lodge here (**Pugu Hills**), though you can visit just for the day but still need to make a reservation for this with the lodge (see page 44).

Pugu Kaolin Mine and the Bat Caves

A further 3-4 km on from the Pugu Hills Reserve is Pugu Kaolin mine, which was established by the Germans in the early 1900s. Kaolin is a type of fine white clay that is used in the manufacture of porcelain, paper and textiles. The deposits here at Pugu are reputed to be the second largest in the world and should the market for it pick up, the mining of kaolin will clearly constitute a further threat to the survival of the remaining rainforest. If you continue through the mine compound you come to a disused railway tunnel, 100 m long and German built (the railway was re-routed after the discovery of kaolin). On the other side of this are a series of man-made caves housing a huge colony of bats. In the early evening at around 1800 or 1900 (depending on the time of year) the bats begin to fly out of the caves for feeding. It is a remarkable experience to stand in the mouth of the caves surrounded by the patter of wings as huge numbers of bats come streaming past you.

Dar es Salaam listings

For Sleeping and Eating price codes and other relevant information, see pages 12-17.

○ Sleeping

As far as top-grade accommodation is concerned, hotels in Dar es Salaam have improved in recent years and there is excellent international standard accommodation in the city centre, Msasani Peninsula and on the beaches to the north and south of the city. The lower end of the market is reasonable value, although it is always sensible to check the room and the bathroom facilities and enquire what is provided for breakfast. Also check on the security of any parked vehicle. Bear in mind that it is possible to negotiate lower rates, especially if you plan to stay a few days. Most upmarket hotels will ask visitors to pay in foreign currency – this really makes no difference but just check the rates in TSh and US$ against the current exchange rate, and make a fuss if you are charged more than the US$ equivalent of the TSh rate. Increasingly, more and more establishments are accepting credit cards, but this often incurs a commission of around 8-15%. In the middle and lower range it is usually possible to pay in TSh, and this is an advantage if money is changed at the favourable bureau rate. VAT at 20% was officially introduced in 1998 and is added to all service charges, though this is usually included in the bill.

Dar es Salaam *p22, maps p30 and p37*
The listings below are split between the city centre and the Msasani Peninsula. Msasani is the European side of town and is where most of the nice hotels can be found.

City centre
$$$$ Kilimanjaro Hotel Kempinski,
Kivukoni Front, T022-213 1111,
www.kempminski-dar essalaam.com.
Occupying a commanding position in the centre of the city overlooking the harbour, this new hotel offers 5-star luxury with contemporary decor and excellent restaurants. A large 5-storey building enclosed in blue glass, it has 180 rooms with all the facilities you'd expect of a top class business hotel. Prices start at US$310 for a de luxe room. There's also a spa, a beautiful swimming pool on the 1st floor and a gym. The **Level 8** nightclub has live music and stunning views over the city. Despite all this, it's slightly lacking in character and service is efficient but impersonal.

$$$$ Southern Sun Hotel, Garden Av, T022-213 7575, www.southernsun.com. The former Holiday Inn, this is one of the nicest hotels in Dar town centre, conveniently located next to the Botanical Gardens (their peacocks regularly fly into the hotel's gardens) and close to the National Museum. 152 well- equipped rooms with Wi-Fi access, a business centre, gym, swimming pool and a popular restaurant and bar (see Eating, page 44). Recommended for its relaxing ambience and friendly and helpful staff.

$$$ Heritage Motel, Kaluta/Bridge St, T022-211 7471, www.heritagemotel.co.tz. Easy to locate in the city centre, this new hotel in a tall, yellow building is conveniently located for the Zanzibar ferry terminal, and is excellent value for money. It has comfortable, spotless rooms (although single rooms are cramped). At the time of visiting, there was a noisy building site next door.

$$$ Palm Beach, 305 Ali Hassan Mwinyi Rd, opposite the junction with Ocean Rd, T022-213 0985, www.pbhtz.com. Stylish art deco hotel, completely refurbished, a little away from the centre of town. Cool and modern decor, 32 rooms, Wi-Fi available, airy bar and restaurant. Popular beer garden with BBQ.

$$$ Peacock Hotel, Bibi Titi Mohamed St, T022-212 0334, www.peacock-hotel.co.tz. Well run and centrally located modern hotel with 69 rooms, with a/c and TV, in a tower block. Great views of downtown Dar from the restaurant on the top floor, which serves good food with occasional theme nights. The unmistakable building was recently 'cocooned' in blue glass to make it cooler inside.

$$$ Peacock Hotel – Millenium Towers, 10 km north of the city on Ali Hassan Mwinyi Rd, (New Bagomoyo Rd), part of the Millennium Towers shopping centre, T022-277 3431, www.peacock-hotel.co.tz. In a glass tower block with ultra modern decor and facilities, all 60 rooms have a/c, satellite TV and internet access. The executive suites are twice the size of the standard rooms, and the junior suites have an extra spare bedroom, both for only US$20 more. Swimming pool, gym, 2 restaurants and bars. A smart business hotel near the **Makumbusho Village Museum** and **Mwenge Craft Market**.

$$$ Protea Hotel Courtyard, Ocean Rd, T022- 213 0130, www.proteahotels.com/courtyard. A quality small hotel with good facilities, a bit more character than some of the larger hotels and with excellent food and service. Standard, superior and de luxe rooms, with a/c, TV and minibar. Wi-Fi, bar, restaurant and pool.

$$$ Royal Palm, Ohio St, T022-211 2416, www. moevenpick-daressalaam.com. Part of the Moevenpick chain, this hotel has conference and banqueting facilities, a shopping arcade and recreation centre, an outdoor swimming pool and lovely gardens. The 230 recently renovated rooms all have a/c and mod cons. The best rooms are at the rear. There's a British Airways office and several restaurants, a coffee shop and a bakery. Wi-Fi available.

$$ Luther House Hotel, on the corner of Sokoine Dr and Pamba Rd, T022-212 0734, luther@simbanet.com, behind the Lutheran church on the waterfront. Central and in considerable demand, so it's necessary to book. Simple freshly painted rooms with basic shower and toilet, TVs and a/c. The Dar Shanghai restaurant is on the ground floor (see Eating, page 45).

$$ Riki Hill Hotel, Kleist Sykes St, west of Mnazi Mmoja Park, T022-218 1820, www.rikihotel.com. 40 rooms in a smart white block several storeys high, comfortable a/c rooms with bathrooms. Restaurant with very good à la carte food, bar and shops, 24-hr bureau de change. Will arrange a free pick up from the airport.

$$ Valley View Hotel, on the corner of Congo St and Matumba A St, T022-218 4556, www. valleyview-hotel.co.tz. A bit out of the way, off Morogoro Rd, a turning opposite United Nations Rd, about 1 km from the intersection with Bibi Titi Mohamed St. A friendly hotel in a neat white and stone building with 41 slightly dated rooms with a/c, TVs, fridge and 24 hr room service. Buffet breakfast.

$ Econolodge, corner of Libya St and Band St, T022-211 6048/50, econolodge@raha.com. A plain but functional place with sparsely furnished, clean self-contained rooms, the cheaper ones have fans, the more expensive have a/c. Small TV lounge. Price includes continental breakfast. Cheapest double US$21.

$ Jambo Inn, Libya St, T022-211 4293, www.jamboinnhotel.com. Centrally located reasonable budget option popular with backpackers. With reliable hot water and working fans, the 28 rooms are self-contained. Rates are as low as US$20 for a double and for a little more you can get a/c. The affordable restaurant serves Indian food (no booze), fresh juice and ice cream; if you are staying in the hotel you get 10% off meals. Internet café downstairs.

$ Safari Inn, Band St, T022-211 9104, safari-inn@lycos.com. Very central, similar to the nearby Jambo Inn, fairly simple but sound. 40 rooms, only 3 with a/c, in a square concrete block down an alleyway (there are security guards are at the entrance). Continental breakfast is included but there's no restaurant. Doubles are US$20 and a single is US$15.

$ YWCA, corner of Azikiwe St and Ghana Av, T022-213 5457, ywca.tanzania@africa online.co.tz, and the YMCA, T022-212 1196, are 1 block apart across Maktaba St. (The YWCA is above the Tanzania Post Bank on Azikiwe St). Both offer simple, clean and cheap accommodation with mosquito nets and fans. Men and women are accepted in both establishments.

Msasani Peninsula *map p37*

$$$$ Hotel Sea Cliff, northern end of the peninsula, Toure Dr, T022-260 03807, www.hotelseacliff.com. Stylish hotel with whitewashed walls and thatched makuti roofing set in manicured grounds. 94 spacious and modern a/c rooms, most with ocean view, and 20 more units in garden cottages, all with satellite TV. Coral Cliff and Ngalawa bars, Calabash Restaurant, and the beautifully positioned Karambezi café bar over the bay. Also has a health club, gift shop, casino, bowling alley and shopping centre. One of the most luxurious hotels in Dar.

$$$$ Oyster Bay Hotel, Toure Dr, T022-260 0530, www.theoysterbayhotel.com. This beautifully chic boutique hotel has recently opened, with 8 stylish bedrooms facing the Indian Ocean. Its British owners also own **Beho Beho** in Selous and place the same emphasis on luxury and relaxation. There's a quiet lawned garden with swimming pool and outdoor eating terrace and the interior is furnished with a mix of contemporary and antique African crafts. Rates are from US$300 per person full board.

$$$ Colosseum Hotel, Haille Selassie Rd, T022-266 6655, www.colosseumtz.com. 42 rooms with a/c, plasma TVs and internet. Guests have free use of the sports facilities, which include a 20 m pool, a gym on 2 floors and 2 squash courts, and can then visit the exotic Cleopatra Spa to help soothe away the aches and pains afterwards. There's a pizzeria and a continental restaurant.

$$$ Coral Beach Hotel, Coral La, T022-260 1928, www.coralbeach-tz.com. A new wing to this hotel opened in Jan 2009, with smart, boutique style rooms, far nicer than those in the old wing. The lobby is bright and breezy; a restaurant and bar overlook the pool set in slightly unkempt gardens, and there's a business centre, gym, sauna and jacuzzi.

$$$ Golden Tulip, Toure Dr, T022-260 0288, www.goldentulipdaressalaam.com. The best thing about this hotel is the huge infinity pool that faces the ocean, set in lovely gardens, which non-residents can use for US$7. The **Maasai Grill** serves good brunches at weekends. The hotel itself looks quite smart from the lobby, but the rooms are tired and shabby. All 91 rooms have TV, a/c and minibar. The Presidential Suite has an exercise bike.

$$$ Peninsula Seaview Hotel, Chuibay Rd, T0787-330888 (mob), www.peninsulasea viewhotel.com. 12 modern en suite bedrooms with TV, Wi-Fi, fridge and fans (no mosquito nets). Food is available at **O'Willie's Irish Whiskey Tavern** on the ground floor with a restaurant terrace outside near the beach, although a sign warns not to walk on the shore without an *askari* (guard).

$$ Q Bar and Guest House, off Haile Selassie Rd, behind the Morogoro Stores, T0754-282474 (mob), www.qbardar.com. 20 comfortable, if a little noisy, rooms in a smart 4 storey block. All have a/c, fridge, bathroom, cool tiled floors and Tingatinga paintings on the walls. Also offer 6 dorm beds for US$12 each. A friendly and popular expat venue with live music and DJs. The bar and restaurant has 3 pool tables, a big screen for watching sport, and plenty of draught beer and cocktails (see Eating, page 46). Separate dining room for guests on the 2nd floor, breakfast included.

Around Dar *p35*
Southern beaches

$$$$ Amani Beach Hotel, 30 km south from the Kigamboni ferry, or air transfers can be arranged from Dar by the resort, T0754-410033 (mob), www.amanibeach.com for online information and reservations. Quality hotel, with a/c, en suite rooms in 10 individual whitewashed cottages decorated with African art, and with garden terraces and hammocks where breakfast is delivered. Swimming pool, tennis courts, horse riding, restaurant, bar, conference facilities and TVs. Set in 30 ha of tropical woodland around a wide bay. Rates are from US$250 per person full board.

$$$$ Ras Kutani, T022-213 4802, www.ras kutani.com. 28 km further south of Kigamboni ferry, 2-hr road journey or a short charter flight from Dar es Salaam arranged by the resort. This resort is small and intimate with only 9 luxurious cottages, 4 suites and a family house beautifully decorated, in a superb location on a hill overlooking the ocean and the wide arch of white sandy isolated beach and freshwater lagoon.

Windsurfing, swimming pool, watersports and snorkelling available but no diving. All rates are full board and are about US$400 per person, resident rates are considerably lower with specials on weekdays.

$$ Kipepeo, Kipepeo Beach next to the **Sunrise Beach Resort** (above), near the village of Mjimwema, 7 km south of the Kigamboni ferry, T 0754-276178 (mob), www.kipepeovillage.com. 20 rustic beach huts built on stilts in a grove of coconut palms with en suite bathrooms. Plenty of space for vehicles and camping (separate hot showers). Overlanders can leave vehicles for a small daily fee while they go to Zanzibar. Very good food and drinks are served on the beach or at the beach bar. A relaxed and affordable option close to the city. Camping US$ 5 per person, basic beach bandas US$25, huts from US$65 including full English breakfast. Recommended.

$$ South Beach Resort, 8 km south of the Kigamboni ferry, Mjimwema,T022-282 0666, www.southbeachresort-tz.com. A brash new resort with a large swimming pool and jacuzzi set in a huge paved area with an outdoor disco, pool tables, shisha lounge and **Whisky Shack** bar. 36 en suite rooms in a characterless block overlooking the pool. The camping ground is shadeless and a long walk from facilities. Day passes are available – Mon-Fri US$4, Sat-Sun US$6, with fines if you bring in your own food or fail to wear your wristband 'tag' which proves payment.

$$ Sunrise Beach Resort, Kipepeo Beach near Mjimwema, 7 km south of Kigamboni ferry, T022-550 7038, www.sunrisebeachresort.co.tz. Characterless 2-storey bandas with balconies and bathrooms, thatched restaurant and bar, Wi-Fi zones, sun loungers on the beach, watersports including jet skiing, quad bikes available for hire. Far better option for camping than the neighbouring **South Beach Resort**, tents are available for US$15 with decent ablutions blocks nearby.

$ Mikadi Beach, 2 km from the Kigamboni ferry, T0754-370269 (mob), www.mikadi beach.com. Recently upgraded by new management, this popular campsite in a grove of coconut palms is right on the beach. Secure parking, clean ablutions, 12 simple double bandas, a swimming pool and a very good bar that gets busy at the weekends. Day rates US$4. For a small fee you can park vehicles here whilst you visit Zanzibar.

Northern beaches

Note It is unsafe to walk along the beach between the northern hotels. The hotels' private beaches are watched by security guards and at the end of the beaches are signs warning guests of the danger of mugging – take heed.

$$$ Beachcomber Hotel, Mbezi Beach, T022-264 7772/4, www.beachcomber.co.tz. Rather concrety development, a/c rooms with TV, minibar and phone. Swahili decor, health club with sauna, steambath and massage, watersports facilities and swimming pool. Offer a free shuttle between the hotel and the airport.

$$$ Kunduchi Resort, Kunduchi, T0748-612231 (mob), www.kunduchiresort.com. Very elegantly decorated modern rooms with a/c, TV and minibar, a mixture of African and Islamic-style architecture and decor for main service areas. Bar, pool bar, excellent restaurants serving continental, seafood and Japanese food, swimming pool, tennis and squash courts, gym, beach with palms and flowers, live music at weekends, watersports facilities and trips to off-shore islands. The **Wet n Wild Water Park** is just next door.

$$$ White Sands, Mbezi Beach, T022-264 7620/6, www.hotelwhitesands.com. Offers 88 sea-facing rooms in thatched villas with TVs, a/c and minibar, and 28 apartments for short and long term lets. Swimming pool, gym, beauty centre and watersports including a PADI dive centre. Several restaurants, one off which (Indian) is superb, and bars. **Water World Waterpark** is adjacent to the hotel. Free shuttle service into the city.

$$ Bahari Beach, Kunduchi, T022-265 0352, www.twiga.ch/tz/bahari.htm. With renovations planned at the time of writing, this hotel has self-contained accommodation in thatched rondavaals with a/c and TV. There's a large bar and restaurant area under the high thatched roofing (limited menu but good food). Swimming pool with bar, band at the weekends and public holidays, traditional dancing Wed night, sandy beach, garden surroundings, gift shop, tour agency and watersports centre. Reports welcome.

$$ Jangwani Sea Breeze Resort, Mbezi Beach, T022-264 7215, www.jangwani.org. 34 a/c rooms with flatscreen TVs and en suite bathrooms. Swimming pool set in pretty gardens with lots of flowering shrubs, right on the beach. 2 other pools (1 just for toddlers), watersports, gym, go-karting, 3 restaurants, pool bar, barbecues and live music at the weekends. Can organize excursions, free shuttle to town centre.

$ Silver Sands, Kunduchi, T022-265 0567, www.silversands.netfirms.com. Pleasant old hotel with restaurant, bar and basic accommodation, some rooms have fans and are cheaper than those with a/c. The weekends attract a number of day visitors when a band plays on the terrace. The food is good and not badly priced. There is also a campsite with a well-maintained ablutions block and it is possible to pitch your tent right on the beach. You can leave a vehicle here while you make a trip to Zanzibar.

Kisarawe and Pugu Hills Forest Reserve *p38*

$$ Pugu Hills, Pugu Hills Forest Reserve, 35 km south of Dar, T0754-56 5498 (mob), www.puguhills.com. 4 smart bamboo huts erected above the forest floor on poles, with hardwood floors and Swahili furnishings. Swimming pool, fabulously rustic restaurant offering snacks and 4 dishes a day including one vegetarian dish, and lovely nature trails through the forest (non-residents have to pay a US\$30 fee for hiking in the reserve). The resort can also arrange visits to a local cattle market. Camping available, US\$7 per person.

Eating

Most of the hotels, including those on the beach out of town, have restaurants and bars. While the city centre has a fair number of good places to eat, many of these are only open during the day, cater for office workers and do not serve alcohol. The best places for dinner and evening drinks are out of the centre on the Msasani Peninsula.

Dar es Salaam *p22, maps p30 and p37*
City centre

Baraza Bar & Grill, Southern Sun Hotel, see Sleeping, above. A deservedly popular restaurant serving a mix of Swahili and continental food, including pastas, curries, grills, seafood and vegetarian dishes. Outdoor terrace onto pool area and a relaxed bar.

Istana, Ali Hassan Mwinyi Rd, opposite Caltex petrol station, a few kilometres out of the city on the Bagamoyo Rd, T022-276 1348. Specializes in Malaysian cuisine. Theme nights throughout the week, Chinese on Tue, meat grill on Wed, satay buffet on Thu, etc. Specialities include *roti canai*, puffed bread filled with meat, chicken and apples and served with hot curries. Good value all you can eat buffets. Open kitchen, tables in the garden, play area with staff to look after children.

Oriental, Kilimanjaro Hotel Kempinski, see Sleeping, above. Open Tue-Sun. Smart, 1st floor restaurant serving a varied Southeast Asian menu with an excellent wine list and impeccable service. Bookings advised.

Sawasdee, top floor of **New Africa Hotel**, Azikwe St, T022-211 7050. Exceptionally good and very authentic Thai food, wonderful harbour views, buffet on Tue and Fri.

Serengeti and **L'Oliveto**, Royal Palm Hotel, see Sleeping, above. **Serengeti** open daily, **L'Oliveto** open Mon-Sat. Upmarket Italian restaurants, reservations recommended and you need to dress up. At the Serengeti there are themed nights every day of the week: Mediterranean on Mon, Italian on Tue, Oriental on Wed, seafood on Thu, popular fondue night on Fri, Tex-Mex on Sat and Indian on Sun. Serve good value buffet lunches with freshly made pasta or salads.

Chef's Pride Restaurant, virtually opposite **Jambo Inn Hotel**, on road between Libya St and Jamhuri St. Closed evenings. Good food at excellent prices, fast service. Italian, Chinese, Indian and local dishes available.

Mediterraneo, Kawe Beach off Old Bagamoyo Rd, midway between the city and the northern beaches, T022-261 8359. Italian pastas, salads and Chinese, occasional live music and Swahili-style buffets. On Sat afternoon there is a barbecue from 1200-2000. Overlooks the ocean, a good place for kids.

Sichuan Restaurant, Bibi Titi Mohamed St, T022-215 0548. Excellent and authentic Chinese restaurant. Most main course dishes are around US$5, and there is a large range to choose from. Plenty of vegetarian options.

Chinese Restaurant, basement of **NIC**, Samora Av. Good, inexpensive Chinese cuisine, also African and some continental dishes. Has been going some 30 years.

City Garden Restaurant, corner of Garden Av and Pamba St, T022-213 4211. African, Indian and Western meals, buffets at lunch-time, excellent juices, tables are set in garden, good service and consistently popular, especially at lunchtime. A new branch has opened on Bridge St. Highly recommended.

Cynics' Café and Wine Bar, in the TDFL building opposite the **Royal Palm Hotel**. Open Mon-Thu until 1800, Fri until 2100. Fresh pastries, salads, sandwiches, wine by the glass, beer and coffee.

Dar Shanghai, behind the Swiss Air office in Luther House Hotel, Sokoine Dr, T022-213

4397. Chinese and Tanzanian menus, canteen-style atmosphere. The food's not brilliant but it's quick and filling. No booze but soft drinks.

Debonair's and **Steer's**, corner of Ohio St and Samora Av, T022-212 2855. Quality South African chains. **Debonair's** serves pizza and salads, while **Steer's** offers burgers, ribs and chips. Also in the Steer's Complex is **Hurry Curry**, an Indian takeaway, **Chop Chop, Chinese**, and a coffee shop. Eat at plastic tables in a/c surroundings.

Garden Food Court, on the 2nd floor of the Haidery Plaza, Kisutu St. Daily 1100-2300. Here you'll find the **Red Onion**, a fairly formal Indian and Pakistani restaurant serving good value lunchtime buffets for US$8; **Natasha Spiced Chicken** for barbecued fast food; and the **Coffee Bud** for snacks and drinks. Food can be taken out of each restaurant and eaten on the outside terrace.

Jambo Inn, Libya St, T022-211 0711. Excellent cheap Indian menu, huge inflated chapattis like air-cushions, also Chinese and European dishes. Outside and inside dining .

Ice cream parlours **Sno-cream**, Mansfield St. An old-fashioned ice cream parlour serving excellent ice cream. Incredibly elaborate sundaes with all the trimmings.

Msasani Peninsula *map p37*

Addis in Dar, 35 Ursino St, off Migombani St/Old Bagamoyo Rd in the Oyster Bay area, near the site of the new US Embassy, T0713-266299 (mob). Open Mon-Sat 1200-1430, 1800-2300. Small and charming Ethiopian restaurant with an outside terrace. Plenty of choice for vegetarians. It is wise to drop in and book ahead.

Azuma, 1st floor at **The Slipway**, T022-260 0893. Open Tue-Fri for dinner, Sat-Sun for lunch and dinner. Japanese and Indonesian restaurant, authentic cuisine with good views over the bay. Very good sushi. If you book ahead, the chef will come out from the kitchen and prepare food at your table.

Fishmonger, upstairs, Sea Cliff Village Food Court, T0754-30 4733 (mob). Excellent fish and seafood from US$12-20, nice outdoor terrace. Non-fishy options are limited.

Hot (in Africa), off Haile Selassie Rd, T0784-839607 (mob). Afro-European food, some of the most inventive cuisine in Dar, traditional roast lunches on a Sun, very trendy decor and a good atmosphere.

Karambezi, Hotel Sea Cliff, see Sleeping, above, T0787-044555 (mob). Beautiful setting on wooden decking overlooking the ocean. Good selection of wines and a varied menu with pizzas, pastas, seafood and grills. Treat yourself to the seafood platter for 2, for US$46.

Oyster Bay Grill, Oyster Bay Shopping Centre, T022-260 0133. Daily 1800-2300. Very elegant and some of the best food in Dar, specializing in steak, seafood and fondue. Average price with wine US$30 per head, much more if you go for the lobster thermidor. Huge range of international wines, whisky and cigar bar, jazz music, outside terrace and more formal fancy tables inside. Accepts credit cards.

Coral Ridge Spur, Sea Cliff Village Food Court, T0752-201745 (mob). South African steak and ribs chain, geared up for families with a play area, Wild West themed decor, big portions and help-yourself salad bar. The meat is good but if you have eaten at a **Spur** elsewhere in Africa there are no surprises.

L'Arca di Noe', Kimweri Av, T0713-601 282 (mob). Open Wed-Mon. Italian pastas, seafood, pizzas from US$5, range of desserts, wide selection of wines, pleasant atmosphere. Wed night is an all you can eat buffet with 26 different pastas and sauces, and on Thu you get a free glass of wine with every pizza.

La Trattoria Jan, Kimweri Av, T0754-282969 (mob). Excellent Italian cuisine, ice creams, open air seating at the rear, pleasant atmosphere and good value. The pizzas are some of the best in town, takeaway available.

Mashua Bar and Grill, at The Slipway, T022-260 0893. Open evenings only. Grills, burgers, salads and pizza. Offers ocean views and live music and dancing on Thu.

Q Bar and Guest House, see Sleeping, above. Open daily 1700 until late, happy hour 1700-1900. The bar has 3 pool tables, a big screen for watching sport, pub grub and plenty of draft beer and cocktails. Live music on Fri and Sat is 1970s soul night.

Shooter's Grill, 86 Kimweri Av, Namanga, T0754-304733 (mob). Very good steaks, ladies get a free glass of wine on Wed and men get a free beer with every T-bone steak sold on a Thu. Live music on Sun, good atmosphere.

Sweet Eazy, Oyster Bay Shopping Centre, Toure Dr, T0755-754074 (mob). Open daily until midnight, happy hour 1700-1900 and all night on Fri. Cocktail bar and restaurant, African and Thai cuisine. Jazz band on Sat.

The Pub, at The Slipway, T022-260 0893. International food, mainly French and Italian in an English-style pub setting, also serves burgers, sandwiches and grills, draft beer and there are good Sun roast lunch specials.

The Terrace, at The Slipway, T022-260 0893. Open Mon-Sat. Italian cuisine and barbecued grills and seafood. Moorish painted arches and outside dining area.

Java Lounge, Sea Cliff Village Food Court, T0748-467149 (mob). Very good service, outdoor deck, range of cocktails and 20 different coffees. Good breakfasts, light meals.

L'Epi d'Or, Samora Av and Sea Cliff Village, T022-213 6006. Mon-Sat 0700-1900. Coffee shop and bakery serving very good sandwiches with imaginative fillings, cappuccino and fresh juice, croissants, pastries and salads.

Around Dar p35
Southern beaches

Mikadi Beach, see Sleeping, above. A great spot on the beach for weekend lunch or all-day breakfasts if you want to escape the city. Speciality alcoholic slushies and a varied menu including fish and chips, home-made burgers, steak sandwiches, vegetarian crêpes and a seafood platter. Day rate of US$4 covers use of the swimming pool next to the shore.

🎵 Bars and clubs

Dar es Salaam *p22, maps p30 and p37*
There are few nightclubs as such in Dar, though many of the hotels and restaurants mentioned above crank it up late in the evening with live music or a DJ, especially at weekends when tables are cleared away for dancing. Some discos are in attractive outdoor settings. Those hotels and restaurants that have regular discos and/or live music are notably **Jangwani Sea Breeze Resort**, and **White Sands Hotel** on the northern beaches; **South Beach Resort** on the southern beaches; **O'Willie's Irish Whisky Tavern** at the Peninsula Sea View Hotel; and the **Q bar** on the Msasani Peninsula. In the city centre, **Level 8** cocktail bar on the 8th floor of the Kilimanjaro Hotel Kempinski, Kivukoni, T022- 213 1111, provides mesmerizing views of downtown Dar at night and occasional live jazz

Club Bilicanas, Mkwepu St, T 0788-904169 (mob). Open every night until around 0400. Entry at weekends is US$23 per person (half of this is redeemable against food and drink). Reopened in Jan 2009 after an extensive 2 year renovation programme, this is far and away the most popular club in Dar. It has been imaginatively designed, with a VIP lounge, 7 bars and glass decor, and has all the effects you'd expect from a world-class night club. Drink prices are reasonable and the place is fully a/c.

🎭 Entertainment

Dar es Salaam *p22, maps p30 and p37*
Casinos
Las Vegas Casino, corner of Upanga Rd and Ufukoni Rd, T022-211 6512. Roulette, poker, blackjack, vingt-et-un and slot machines.

There are also casinos at the **Kilimanjaro Hotel Kempinski,** T022-213 1111 (open until 0400) and **Hotel Sea Cliff**, T022-260 0380.

Cinema
Visitors seldom go to the cinema, which is a pity as the audience reaction makes for an exciting experience. Programmes are in the newspapers or monthly guides such as *Dar Life* and *Dar es Salaam Guide*. The cinemas show mostly Indian, martial arts or adventure films. Entrance is about US$4.
British Council, Ohio St, T022-211 6574. Shows films fairly regular film on a Wed.
Century Cinemax, in the Mlimani City Shopping Mall near the university, T022-277 3053. New complex, discounts on Thu.
New World Cinemas, New Bagamayo Rd, T022-277 1409. Discounts on Tue.

Live music
Concerts of classical music by touring artists are presented by the **British Council**, the **Alliance Française** and occasionally other embassies. African bands and artists and Indian groups play regularly at the hotels and restaurants especially at weekends. Look for announcements in the *Dar es Salaam Guide*, and *What's Happening in Dar es Salaam*.

Theatre
British Council, Ohio St. Occasionally presents productions, check the papers.
Little Theatre, Haile Selassie Rd, off Ali Hassan Mwinyi Rd, next door to the Protea Apartments, T0784-277388 (mob), daressalaamplayers@raha.com. Presents productions on an occasional basis, perhaps half a dozen a year, usually drama and comedy and 1 musical a year. Very popular, particularly the Christmas pantomime.

🛍 Shopping

Dar es Salaam *p22, maps p30 and p37*
There are shops along Samora Av (electrical goods, clothing, footwear) and on Libya St (clothing and footwear). Supermarkets, with a wide variety of imported foods and wines, are on Samora Av between Pamba Av and

Azikawe St; on the corner of Kaluta St and Bridge St; opposite Woolworth's on Garden Av; in Shopper's Plaza; and in the Oyster Bay Hotel Shopping Mall. The new Mlimani City Shopping Mall, Sam Nujoma Rd near Dar University is also home to a huge **Shoprite** supermarket. A popular location for buying fruit and vegetables is the market on Kinondoni Rd, just north of Msimbuzi Creek.

The Namanga shops are at the corner of Old and New Bagamoyo Rd, and are basically stalls selling household supplies and food; there's a good butcher's towards the back. **Manzese Mitumba Stalls**, Morogoro Rd, Manzese, has great bargains for second- hand clothing and Uhuru St has several *kanga* shops (the traditional wrap-arounds worn by women) usually for little more than US$3. **Ilala Market**, on Uhuru St, sells vegetables, fresh and dried fish and second- hand clothing. Fresh fish and seafood can be bought at the **Fish Market** on Ocean Rd, just past the Kigamboni ferry.

Shopping centres and department stores

Haidery Plaza, at the corner of Upanga Rd and Kisutu St in the city centre. A small shopping centre that as well as shops has an internet café and a popular food court.
Mayfair Plaza, opposite TMJ Hospital, Old Bagomoyo Rd, Oyster Bay, www.may fairplaza.co.za. This centre has a number of quality shops, including upmarket clothes and shoe shops, jewellers, dry cleaners, banks, pharmacies and a branch of **Shoprite**, plus coffee shops and a food court.
Mlimani City Shopping Mall, San Nujoma Rd, near the university. Dar's latest shopping centre with a huge cinema complex, one of the biggest **Shoprite** supermarkets in Tanzania, and a plethora of smaller shops covering everything from clothes to electronics.
Oyster Bay Hotel Shopping Centre, see Sleeping, page 42. Supermarket, internet café, and gift and art shops. There are plans to renovate this centre.
Sea Cliff Village, Hotel Sea Cliff, see Sleeping, page 41. Has a branch of the excellent bookshop **A Novel Idea** (see below), a French bakery, and a good shop upstairs called **Mswumbi** that sells fresh coffee beans. There are 'day rooms' for rent here – bedrooms that are only let out during the day for people who have returned to Dar from safari andare not flying out until the evening (contact the hotel). There's also a vastly overpriced supermarket catering for expats.
Shoppers' Plaza, Old Bagamoyo Rd, on the Msasani Peninsula. Has a good variety of shops, including a large supermarket. The Arcade nearby, has a travel agency, boutiques, hairdresser, nail technician, glass and framing shop, and restaurants.
The Slipway complex, on the Msasani Peninsula, facing Msasani Bay. Expensive, high quality goods can be found here. Another branch of **Shoprite**, an internet café, a craft market, a hair and beauty salon, several restaurants and a branch of Barclay's Bank with an ATM. There are also a few 'day rooms'. To book these contact Coastal Air, T022-260 0893, www.slipway.net.
Woolworths, in the New PPF Towers building on Ohio St. The only department store in Dar, this is a South African clothing store very similar to the UK's Marks & Spencer.

Bookshops

Second-hand books can be found at the stalls on Samora Av, on Pamba St (off Samora), on Maktaba St and outside Tancot House, opposite Luther House. Most of these also sell international news magazines such as *Time*, *Newsweek*, *New African*, etc.
A Novel Idea, branches at **The Slipway**, Msasani Peninsula, at the **Hotel Sea Cliff**, and on the corner of Ohio St and Samora Av, T022-260 1088, www.anovelidea-africa.com. The best bookshop in Dar by far, this is

perhaps the most comprehensive bookshop in East Africa with a full range of new novels, coffee table books, maps and guide books.

Other bookshops are the **Tanzanian Bookshop**, Indira Gandhi St, leading from the Askari Monument; and **Tanzania Publishing House**, Samora Av. Both have only limited selections.

Curios and crafts
Traditional crafts, particularly wooden carvings, are sold along Samora Av to the south of the Askari Monument. Good value crafts can be purchased from stalls along Ali Hassan Mwinyi Rd near the intersection with Haile Selassie Rd and, in particular, at **Mwenge**, along Sam Njoma Rd, close to the intersection with Ali Hassan Mwinyi Rd. This is the best place for handicrafts in Dar, and for ethnographia from all over Tanzania and further afield (notably the Congo). There are a large number of shops and stalls offering goods at very reasonable prices and you can watch the carvers at work. The market is 10 km or about 30 mins from the town centre towards the northern beaches, easily reached by *dala-dala*. It is just around the corner from the *dala-dala* stand.

More expensive, quality modern wood products can be obtained from **Domus**, in The Slipway complex, which also houses **The Gallery**, selling wood products as well as paintings by local artists. There is a craft market here selling tablecloths, cushions and beadwork, and a Tingatinga workshop.

▲ Activities and tours

Dar es Salaam *p22, maps p30 and p37*
Athletics
Meetings at the National Stadium, Mandela Rd to the south of the city.

Cricket
Almost entirely a pursuit of the Asian community. There are regular games at week- ends at: **Annadil Burhani Cricket Ground**, off Aly Khan Rd; **Gymkhana Club**, off Ghana Av; **Jangwani Playing Fields**, off Morogoro Rd, in the valley of Msimbazi Creek; and **Leaders Club**, Dahomey Rd, off Ali Hassan Mwinyi Rd.

Diving
Sea Breeze Marine Ltd, White Sands Hotel, T022-264 7620, www.seabreezemarine.org.

Fishing
Marine fishing can be arranged through many of the hotels on the beaches.

Fitness and running
The **Hash House Harriers** meet at 1730 on Mon afternoons, details are available from the British Council, Ohio St, T022-211 6574.
Colosseum Hotel & Fitness Club, Haille Selassie Rd, T022-266 6655. Has a state-of-the-art gym spread over 2 floors, a range of fitness classes, 2 squash courts, a swimming pool and spa. A day pass is US$15 with discounts for multiple days.
The Fitness Centre, off Chole Rd on Msasani Peninsula, T022-260 0786. A gym with weights and also aerobics and yoga classes.
Millenium Health Club, Mahando St, at the north end of Msasani Peninsula, T022-260 2609. Has a gym, aerobics, sauna and beauty parlour.

There are also gyms at the **Hotel Sea Cliff** and **White Sands Hotel**.

Golf
Gymkhana Club, Ghana Av, T022-212 0519. Only guests are permitted to play golf at the club. Costs are around US$28 for 18 holes, you can hire very good quality clubs and shoes . Here, because of a shortage of water, you will be playing on browns not greens.

Sailing
Yacht Club, Chole Rd, Msasani Peninsula, T022-260 0132. Visitors can obtain temporary membership here. The club organizes East

Africa's premier sailing event, the Dar to Tanga (and back) Yacht Race every Dec.

Soccer

The main African pursuit, followed by everyone from the President and the Cabinet down. Matches are exciting occasions, with radios throughout the city tuned to the commentary. Terrace entrance is around US$2 (more for important matches). It is worth paying extra to sit in the stand. There are 2 divisions of the National league, and Dar es Salaam has 2 representatives – **Simba** and **Young Africans** (often called Yanga) – and there is intense rivalry between them. Simba, the best-known Tanzanian club, have their origins in Kariakoo and are sometimes referred to as the 'Msimbazi Street Boys' – they have a club bar in Msimbazi St. Initially formed in the 1920s as 'Eagles of the Night', they changed their name to 'Sunderland FC' in the 1950s. After independence all teams had to choose African names and they became Simba. See www.simbasportsclub.com, for more information.

The 2 main venues for watching soccer:
Karume Stadium, just beyond the Kariakoo area, off Uhuru St.
National Stadium, Mandela Rd to the south of the city. This has recently been renovated. The national team **Taifa Stars** play regularly here, mostly against other African teams.

Swimming

Many of the larger hotels have swimming pools that charge a small fee for non-guests.
Swimming Club, Ocean Rd near Magogoni St. This is the best place to swim in the sea. Otherwise, the best sea beaches are some distance to the north and south of the city.
Water World, next to **White Sands Hotel**, Mbezi Beach. Tue-Sun. US$5 adults, US$4 children. Has several different water slides and games for children.
Wet 'n' Wild, Kunduchi Beach, T022-265 0326. This is an enormous complex largely, though not exclusively, for children. There

are 7 swimming pools with 22 water slides, 2 are very high and 1 twists and turns for 250 m. There is an area for younger children, tennis and squash courts, go-karting, an internet café, hair and beauty parlour, fast food outlets and a main restaurant, and also facilities for watersports on the open ocean, including windsurfing and fishing trips; there is even a qualified diving instructor.

Tour operators

A variety of companies offer tours to the game parks, the islands (Zanzibar, Pemba, Mafia) and to places of historical interest (Kilwa, Bagamoyo). It is well worth shopping around as prices (and degrees of luxury) vary. It is important to find an operator that you like, offers good service, and does not pressure you into booking something.
Bon Voyage Travel, Ohio St, T022-211 8198, www.bonvoyagetz.com.
Cordial Tours, Sokoine Rd T 027-250 6495, www.cordialtours.com.
Easy Travel & Tours, Raha Towers, Bibi Titi Mohamed St, T022-212 3526, T022-212 3842, www.easytravel.co.tz.
Ebony Tours & Safaris, T0773-011153 (mob), www.ebony-safaris.com.
Emslies Travel Ltd, NIC Investment House, 3rd Flr, Samora Av, opposite Royal Palm Hotel, T022-211 4065, www.emsliestravel.biz.
Fortune Travels & Tours Ltd, Jamhuri St, T022-213 8288, www.fortunetz.com.
Hakuna Matata, The Arcade, Old Bagamoyo Rd, T022-270 0231.
Hima Tours & Travel, Simu St, T022-211 1083, www.himatours.com.
Hippo Tours & Safaris, Mwalimu Nyerere Cultural Centre (Nyumba ya Sanaa), T022-212 8662, www.hippotours.com.
Hit Holidays, Bibi Titi Mohamed St (near Rickshaw Travel), T022-211 9024, www.hitholidays.com.
Holiday Africa Tours & Safaris, TDFL Bldg, Ohio St, T022-212 7746.
Interline Travel & Tours, NIC Life House,

Sokoine Dr/Ohio St, T022-213 7433.
Kearsley Travel and Tours, Kearsley House, Indira Gandhi St, T022-211 5026/30, www.kearsley.net.
Leopard Tours, Movenpick Royal Palm Hotel, Ohio St, T022-211 9754/6, www.leopard-tours.com.
Lions of Tanzania Safari & Tours, Peugeot House, Bibi Titi Mohamed Rd, T022-212 8161, www.lions.co.tz.
Luft Travel & Cargo Ltd, GAK Patel Bldg, Maktaba St, T022-213 8843.
Planet Safaris, Ohio St, T022-213 7456, www.planetsafaris.com.
Reza Travel & Tours, Jamhuri St, opposite Caltex Station, T022-213 4458, reza@rezatravel.com.
Rickshaw Travel (American Express Agents), Royal Palm Hotel, Ohio St, T022-211 4094, www.rickshawtravels.com.
Skylink Travel & Tours, TDFL Bldg, Ohio St, opposite Royal Palm Hotel, T022-211 5381; airport, T022-284 2738; Mayfair Plaza, T022-277 3983, www.skylinktanzania.com.
Sykes, Indira Ghandi St, T022-211 5542, www.sykestours.co.uk.
Takims Holidays Tours and Safaris, Mtendeni St, T022-211 0346/8, www.takimsholidays.com.
A Tent with a View Safaris, Zahara Towers, Zanaki St, T022-211 0507, www.saadani.com, www.selouslodge.com, www.safariscene.com.
Walji's Travel Bureau, Zanaki St/Indira Ghandi St corner, T022-211 0321, www.waljistravel.com.
Wild Thing Safaris, corner of Makunganya St and Simu St, www.wildthingsafaris.com.

☺ Transport

Dar es Salaam *p22, maps p30 and p37*
Air
For air charter operators see page 9. Domestic flight schedules change regularly and it's always best to check with the airlines before making plans. It's also necessary to reconfirm

your bookings a day or so before flying since timings often change. **Precision Air** depart from the International Terminal at Dar airport, the other airlines all depart from the domestic terminal. Most domestic flights have a baggage limit of 15 kg per person.
Air Tanzania, T022-211 8411, www.air tanzania.com, has 2 daily flights from Dar to **Zanzibar** at 0900 and 1600 (25 mins); a daily flight to **Kilimanjaro** at either 0910 or 2000 (55 mins) depending on the day of the week; and 2 daily flights to **Mwanza** at 0700 and 1600 (1 hr 30 mins).
  Coastal Air, T022-284 2700/1, www. coastal.cc, has a scheduled service from Dar to **Arusha** (2 hrs) via **Zanzibar** daily at 0900. This service continues on to the **Serengeti**. To **Kilwa** (1 hr) via **Mafia Island** (30 mins) at 1500. To **Pemba** at 1400 (1 hr). Flights to **Ruaha** (3 hrs) via **Selous** (30 mins) depart at 0830. There's another daily flight to the Selous at 1430 which stops at all the camps. **Tanga** (1 hr 30 mins) daily via Zanzibar and Pemba at 1400. Flights to **Zanzibar** daily every 1½ hrs from 0730-1530, and 1645 and 1745 (20 mins, US$75).
  Precision Air, T022-213 0800, T022-212 1718, www.precisionairtz.com, flies to **Mwanza** Wed, Fri and Sun at 0810, Mon, Tue, Thu and Sat at 1055 (2 hrs). To **Tabora** (2 hrs) and **Kigoma** (3 hrs 15 mins) Fri-Wed at 1100. To **Zanzibar** daily 0650 and 1320 (20 mins). There are additional flights to Zanzibar on Thu and Fri at 0830, and on Mon, Tue, Wed, Sat and Sun 1100. To **Arusha** daily 0820 and 1320 (1 hr 15 mins). To **Shinyanga** on Mon, Wed, Fri and Sun at 1330 (2 hrs).
  Zanair, T024-223 3768, www.zanair.com, have daily flights from Dar to **Zanzibar** at 0900, 1215, 1645 and 1815; direct to **Pemba** at 1345; and to the **Selous** at 0840.
  Airline offices Air India, Bibi Titi Mohamed St, opposite Peugeot House, T022-215 2642, www.airindia.com. **Air**

Malawi, JM Mall, Samora Av, T022-212 4280, www.airmalawi.com. **Air Tanzania**, ATC Bldg, Ohio St, T022-211 8411, www.airtanzania.com. **British Airways**, based at the Royal Palm Hotel, Ohio St, T022-2113 8202, www.britishhairways.com. **Emirates**, Haidery Plaza, Kisutu St, T022-2116 1003, www.emirates.com. **Ethiopian Airlines**, TDFL Bldg, Ohio St, T022-2117 0635, www.flyethiopia.com. **Gulf Air**, Raha Towers, Bibi Titi Mohamed St/Maktaba St, T022-2137 8526, www.gulfairco.com. **Kenya Airways**, Peugeot House, Bibi Titi Mohammed/Ali Hassan Mwinyi Rd, T022-211 9376, www.kenya-airways.com. **KLM**, Peugeot House as above T022-211 3336, www.klm.com. **Oman Air**, airport, T022-213 5660, www.oman-air.com. **Qatar Airways**, Barclays House, Ohio St, T022-211 8870, www.qatarairways.com. **South Africa Airways**, Raha Tower, Bibi Titi Mohammed St, T022-2117 0447, www.flysaa.com. **Swiss Air**, Luther House, Sokoine Dr, T022-211 8 8703, www.swiss.com.

Bus

The main bus station is **Ubungo Bus Station** on Morogoro Rd, 6 km from the city centre, which can be reached by bus, *dala-dala* or taxi. Outside on the road is a long line of booking offices. Recommended for safety and reliability is **Scandinavia Express**, which has its own terminal on Nyerere Rd at the corner of Msimbazi St (taxi from the city centre approximately US$2), though all buses also stop at the Ubungo bus station, T022-285 0847, www.scandinaviagroup.com. There is a small airport-style arrival and departure lounge at the terminal with its own restaurant. Buses are speed limited, luggage is securely locked up either under the bus or in overhead compartments, and complimentary video, drinks, sweets and biscuits are offered. Buses depart daily for **Arusha** at 0745, 0830 and 0915 (9 hrs, US$30 luxury service, US$20 standard); **Mbeya** at

0645 and 0745 (12 hrs, US$20); **Tanga** at 0800 (6 hrs, US$8.50), and **Dodoma** at 0915 and 1100 (4 hrs, US$10). **International destinations Mombasa** and **Nairobi** in Kenya, **Kampala** in Uganda and **Lusaka** in Zambia.

Other bus companies include **Dar Express** T0754-373415 (mob) and **Royal Coaches** T022-212 4073.

Car hire

Car hire can be arranged through most of the tour operators. Alternatively try: **Avis**, in the TDFL building, opposite the Royal Palm Hotel, Ohio St, run by Skylink Travel & Tours, T022-211 5381, www.avis.com; **Business Rent a Car**, 16 Kisitu St, T022-212 2852, www.businessrentacar.com; **Green Car Rentals**, Nukrumah St, along Nyerere Rd, T022-218 3718, T0713-227788 (mob), www.greencarstz.com; **Hertz**, airport, T022-211 2967, www.hertz.com; or **Tanzania Rent-A-Car**, airport, T022-212 8062.

Ferry

All ticket offices of the ferry companies with services to **Zanzibar** and **Pemba** are on Sokoine Dr adjacent to the jetty. Ignore the touts who may follow you to the offices to claim credit and take commission. The companies themselves advise travellers to completely ignore them and it is easy enough to book a ticket on your own.

Most ferries are fast and comfortable hydrofoils or catamarans that take on average 90 mins to reach Zanzibar, and the tourist fare is fixed at US$45 one way (including port tax) for all companies. The slow over-night boat back from Zanzibar with **Flying Horse** is US$25. Payment for tickets is in US$ cash. Companies no longer accept TCs.

Services to **Zanzibar and Pemba**: Azam Marine, T022-213 4013, www.azam-marine.com. Australian-built Seabus catamarans that take 1 hr 40 mins to Zanzibar. They depart daily at 0800, 1115, 1330, 1400 and 1600. From Zanzibar to Dar, ferries depart at 0700, 0930, 1330 and 1630. On Tue and Fri they also operate a service from Dar es Salaam to Pemba via Zanzibar at 0730 which arrives in Zanzibar at 0855, departs again at 1000 and arrives in Pemba at 1205. The return boat on Tue and Fri departs Pemba at 1230, arrives in Zanzibar at 1435, departs again at 1630 and arrives in Dar at 1755.

Flying Horse (Africa Shipping Corporation), T022-212 4507. Outward journey to Zanzibar departs at 1200 and takes 2 hrs, the overnight return from Zanzibar departs 2200. For some this return journey is inconvenient as passengers are not let off at Dar until 0600, when Customs open. However, tourists are accommodated in comfortable, a/c compartments, and provided with mattresses to sleep on until 0600. A good option for budget travellers as the fare is only US$20 each way and you save on accommodation for 1 night.

Sea Express, T022-213 7049, www.sea-express.net. Daily ferry from Dar at 0715 which arrives in Zanzibar at 0915, leaving Zanzibar for the return at 1600. On Mon, Wed, Fri and Sun the ferry continues from Zanzibar (departing at 1000) to Pemba where it arrives at 1200, leaving Pemba at 1300 to return. Dar es Salaam to Pemba US$70.

Sea Star, T022-212 4988. Fast service to Zanzibar that takes 1 hr 30 mins, departs Dar at 1030. The return leaves Zanzibar at 0700.

Sepideh, T0713-282365 (mob). Departs Dar at 0700, continuing on to Pemba at 0930 on Sat, Mon and Thu, arriving there at 1300.

Train

The **Central Railway Station** is off Sokoine Dr at the wharf end of the city at the corner of Railway St and Gerezani St, T022-211 7833, www.trctz.com. This station serves the passenger line that runs through the central zone to **Kigoma** on Lake Tanganyika and **Mwanza** on Lake Victoria.

TAZARA Railway Station is at the junction of Mandela Rd and Nyerere Rd, about 5 km from the city centre, T022-286 5187, www.tazara.co.tz. You can book train tickets online. It is well served by *dala-dala* and a taxi from the centre costs about US$5. This line runs southwest to **Iringa** and **Mbeya** and on to **Tunduma** at the Zambia border (24 hrs). It is a broader gauge than the Central and Northern Line.

To Zambia Express trains go all the way to **New Kapiri Mposhi** and this journey takes 40-50 hrs. The local trains, which stop at the Zambian border, are a little slower, and take approximately 23 hrs to get to **Mbeya**. First class cabins on both trains contain 4 berths and second class 6.

⊙ Directory

Dar es Salaam *p22, maps p30 and p37*
Banks
All banks listed have ATMs, though some may only accept Visa cards. **Standard Chartered**, in the Plaza on Sokoine Dr near Askari Monument, and at International House on corner of Garden Av and Shaaban Robert St. **Barclay's**, TDFL Building, Ohio St, and at The Slipway. **CitiBank**, Peugeot House, Bibi Titi Mohammed Rd. **National Bank of Commerce**, Samora Av and corner of Sokoine Dr and Azikiwe St. Bank hours are Mon-Fri 0830-1500, Sat 0830-1130.

Currency exchange Foreign exchange bureaux are to be found in almost every street, and are especially common in the area between Samora Av and Jamhuri St. They are usually open Mon-Fri 0900-1700 and Sat 0900-1300. Some are also open Sun morning. Rates vary and it is worth shopping around. Tanzania's sole agent for American Express is **Rickshaw Travel**, at the Royal Palm Hotel, T022-211 4094, www.rickshaw travels.com, open Mon-Fri all day, Sat-Sun mornings only, will issue TCs to card-holders.

Money transfers Western Union money

transfer is available at the Tanzanian Postal Bank, on Samora Av, and at the General Post Office on Azikiwe St.

Immigration

The immigration office is on the corner of Ohio St and Garden Av, T022-211 2174, open Mon-Fri 0730-1530.

Medical services

Hospitals The main hospital is **Muhimbili Hospital**, off United Nations Rd, northwest of the centre towards Msimbazi Creek, T022-215 1298. **Oyster Bay Medical Clinic**, follow the signs along Haile Selassie Rd, T022-266 7932, is an efficient and accessible small private medical centre. **Aga Khan Hospital**, Ocean Rd at the junction with Ufukoni Rd, T022-2115 1513. All these hospitals are well equipped and staffed. See also **Flying Doctors Society of Africa**, page .

Pharmacies In all shopping centres, and small dispensaries are also found in the main residential areas.

Police

The **main police station** is on Gerazani St near the railway station, T022-211 5507. There are also stations on Upanga Rd on the city side of Selander Bridge, T022-212 0818;

on Ali Hassan Mwinyi Rd at the junction with Old Bagamoyo Rd (Oyster Bay), T022-266 7322/3; and at the port T022-211 6287.

Emergencies For police, ambulance and fire brigade, T112.

Post office

The **main post office** is on Azikiwe St, and it's here that you will find the poste restante. There's a small charge for letters collected. Other offices are on Sokoine Dr, behind the bus stand on Morogoro Rd; and Libya St. Post offices are generally crowded.

Courier services Several branches of the major courier companies around town which will collect. **DHL** at DHL House, 12B Nyerere Rd, T022-286 1000/4, www.africa.dhl.com. **Fedex**, T022-270 1647. **TNT**, T022-212 4585.

Telephone

International calls and faxes can be made from the telecoms office near the main post office on Simu St. There are also many private telephone offices all over town. Hotels will usually charge up to 3 times the actual cost. There are mobile phone shops all over Dar and international calls may well be cheaper if you buy a local phone or pay-as-you-go SIM card.

Contents

Footprint features

Zanzibar & Pemba

Ins and outs → *Phone code: 024.*

Getting there

Immigration The islands that make up the Zanzibar Archipelago – Unguja (usually known as Zanzibar Island), Pemba and numerous smaller islands – lie roughly 35 km off the coast of mainland Tanzania. Whilst still part of Tanzania they are administered autonomously and have their own immigration procedures. Therefore, you will be asked to show your passport to an immigration official on entry and exit and have it stamped in and out. Likewise, your passport is stamped on arrival once back on mainland Tanzania. Note that the agreement between Tanzania, Kenya and Uganda, that allows holders of single entry visas to move freely between all three countries without the need for re-entry permits, also covers travel to Zanzibar. You also require a vaccination certificate for yellow fever to get onto the islands, and this is asked for on arrival at the port or airport.

Travel There are frequent ferries between Dar es Salaam and Stone Town on Zanzibar, from big old slow overnight boats to 90-minute hydrofoils, and how much you pay depends on the level of comfort and how quickly you want to get there (see Dar es Salaam, page 52, for further information). There are less frequent ferry services between Dar and Mkoani on Pemba, of which almost all stop at Zanzibar en route. **Zanzibar's International Airport** ① *T024-223 0213*, is 6 km outside of Stone Town and is equipped to receive small planes from the outskirts of Stone Town, larger jets from Nairobi and further afield, as well as European charter flights. Visitors arriving on Zanzibar from outside Tanzania will be able to obtain a visa on entry. The small airport at Pemba is near Chake Chake and the smaller airlines link Pemba with Dar es Salaam and Zanzibar. There is an international airport departure tax of US$25, and a domestic departure tax of US$5, although these are sometimes included in the price of your flights so check with your airline (the latter is payable in local currency). ▶ *For further details, see Transport, page 85.*

Getting around

Public transport on Zanzibar in the way of buses and *dala-dala* is cheap, with regular services, and the main roads around the island are now all tarmac. The other option is to use reasonably priced transfers in minibuses organized by the tour operators. If you want to drive yourself cars, jeeps and motorbikes can be hired, and for a group of four people, hiring a car can sometimes work out cheaper than paying for individual transfers. There is a vehicle rental office in the Old Post Office in Stone Town or you can go through one of the tour operators (see page 84). You will need an international driver's licence, and recently it has also been necessary to have a Zanzibar Driver's Permit. These are issued by the car hire company or tour operator when you arrange your vehicle and cost US$10-20. Without this permit you may get harassed at the police road blocks on the island, of which there are several, so discuss this with your tour operator. Some of the more exclusive lodges are on the smaller islands. To get to these the lodge will organize a boat transfer. On Pemba, *dala-dala* and the odd bus run up and down the main roads from early morning to early afternoon and their regularity rather depends on how many people want to use them.

Climate

The climate is generally tropical, but the heat is tempered by a sea breeze throughout the year. The average temperature fluctuates between 25-30°C. There are long rains from March to mid-June and short rains in November and December. The hottest time is after

Zanzibar Island

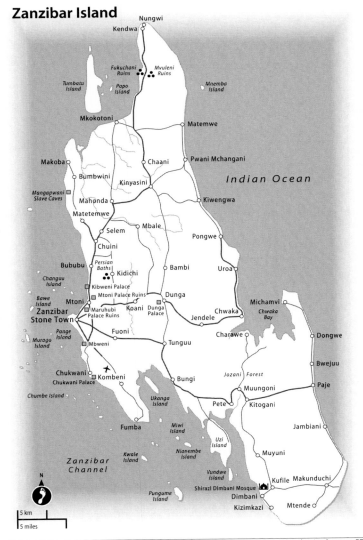

the short rains from December-February, with temperatures up to 34°C at midday. The most comfortable time of year is June-October, with lower temperatures, little rain and plenty of sun, made bearable by the cooling winds from the southeast, known as the *Kusi* or the Southeast Monsoons. From October-March the winds change, blowing from the northeast, and they are known as the *Kaskazi* or the Northeast Monsoons.

Tourist information and maps

The **Zanzibar Tourism Cooperation (ZTC)** ① *T024-223 8630, www.zanzibartourism.net*, is in Livingstone House about 1 km along the road to Bububu, Stone Town. They can arrange all tours of the island. The ZTC also has another **Tourist Information Centre** ① *Creek Rd, T024-223 3430*, at the north end in the Kikoni district, which sells maps of the island but otherwise is not terribly helpful. *The Swahili Coast* is a free bi-monthly publication from Coastal Airlines available from some hotels, tour agencies, a few embassies and airline offices. It lists hotels, restaurants, transport services, etc, and features articles about local events on the islands and along the mainland coast.

The best maps available are produced by **The Zanzibar Gallery** ① *Gizenga St*, in Stone Town; *Illustrated Zanzibar Map* and *Illustrated Pemba Map*, both have extra information about weather, distances and very usefully, *dala-dala* routes. Each costs around US$0.50 and is available from The Gallery and various other outlets in Stone Town and Dar es Salaam. Try the bookshops in Dar such as **A Novel Idea**, see page 48.

Background

The origin of the name Zanzibar is disputed. The Omani Arabs believe it came from *Zayn Zal Barr*, which means 'Fair is the Island'. The alternative origin is in two parts – the early inhabitants of the island were from the mainland and were given the name *Zenj*, a Persian word that is a corruption of *Zangh* meaning negro. The word *bar* meaning 'coast' was added to this to give 'Negro Coast'.

The earliest visitors were Arab traders who brought with them Islam, which has remained the dominant religion on the island. They are believed to have arrived in the eighth century. The earliest remaining building is the mosque at Kizimkazi that dates from about 1100. For centuries the Arabs had sailed with the monsoons down from Muscat and Oman in the Gulf to trade in ivory, slaves, spices, hides and wrought-iron. The two main islands, both of roughly similar size, Unguja (usually known as Zanzibar Island) and Pemba, provided an ideal base, being relatively small islands and thus easy to defend. From here it was possible to control 1500 km of the mainland coast from present day Mozambique up to Somalia. A consequence of their being the first arrivals was that the Arabs became the main landowners.

In 1832 Sultan Seyyid Said, of the Al Busaid dynasty that had emerged in Oman in 1744, moved his palace from Muscat to Zanzibar. Said and his descendants were to rule there for 134 years. In 1822, the Omanis signed the Moresby Treaty that made it illegal for them to sell slaves to Christian powers in their dominions. To monitor this agreement, the United States in 1836 and the British in 1840 established diplomatic relations with Zanzibar, and sent resident consuls to the islands. The slaving restrictions were not effective and the trade continued to flourish. Caravans set out from Bagamoyo on the mainland coast, travelling up to 1500 km on foot as far as Lake Tanganyika, purchasing slaves from local rulers on the way, or, more cheaply, simply capturing them. The slaves, chained together, carried ivory back to Bagamoyo. The name Bagamoyo means 'lay down your heart' for it was here that the slaves would abandon hope of ever seeing their homeland again. They were shipped to the slave market in Zanzibar Town, bought by intermediary traders, who in turn sold them on without any restrictions.

All the main racial groups were involved in the slave trade. Europeans used slaves in the plantations in the Indian Ocean islands, Arabs were the main capturers and traders, and African rulers sold the prisoners taken in battle to the traders. Alas, being sold into slavery was not the worst fate that could befall a captive. If a prolonged conflict led to a glut, the Doe tribe from just north of Bagamoyo would run down excess stocks of prisoners by the simple expedient of eating them. Nevertheless, it is the perception of the African population that the Arabs were mainly responsible.

Cloves had been introduced from Southeast Asia, probably Indonesia, prior to the advent of Sultan Seyyid Said. They flourished in the tropical climate on the fertile and well-watered soils on the western areas of both Zanzibar and Pemba islands. Slaves did the cultivation and harvesting and the Sultan owned the plots: by his death in 1856 he had 45 plantations. Other plantations were acquired by his many children, as well as by numerous concubines and eunuchs from the royal harem. In due course cinnamon, nutmeg, black pepper, cumin, ginger and cardamom were all established, their fragrance was everywhere and Zanzibar became known as the 'Spice Islands'. Slaves, spices and ivory provided the basis of considerable prosperity, mostly in the hands of the Arab community, who were the main landowners, and who kept themselves to themselves and did not intermarry with the Africans.

This was not true of a second group that came from the Middle East to settle on the East African coast, the Shirazis. Intermarriage between Shirazis and Africans gave rise to a coastal community with distinctive features, and a language derived in part from Arabic. This became known as Swahili. In Zanzibar the descendants of this group were known as the Afro-Shirazis. They were not greatly involved in the lucrative slave, spice and ivory trades. They cultivated coconuts, fished and became agricultural labourers. Those Shirazis who did not intermarry retained their identity as a separate group.

Two smaller communities were also established. Indian traders arrived in connection with the spice and ivory trade, and, as elsewhere, settled as shopkeepers, traders, skilled artisans, money-lenders, lawyers, doctors and accountants. The British became involved in missionary and trading activities in East Africa while attempting to suppress the slave trade. And when Germans began trading on the mainland opposite Zanzibar, things needed to be sorted out with the Sultan of Zanzibar, who controlled the 10-mile coastal strip that ran for 1500 km from Mozambique to Somalia. The Germans bought their strip of the coast from the Sultan for £200,000. The British East African Company had been paying the Sultan £11,000 a year for operating in the Kenyan portion. In 1890, Germany allowed Britain to establish a protectorate over Zanzibar in return for Heligoland, a tiny barren island occupied by the British, but strategically placed opposite the mouth of the River Elbe, 50 km from the German coast. In 1895 Britain took over responsibility for its section of the mainland from the British East African Company and agreed to continue to pay the £11,000 a year to the Sultan. The British mainland territory (later Kenya), was administered by a Governor, to whom the British representative in Zanzibar, the Resident, was accountable.

The distinctive feature of Zanzibar as a protectorate (Kenya had become a colony in 1920) was recognized in 1926 when the British Resident was made directly responsible to the Colonial Secretary in London. Germany had by this stage lost control of its section of the mainland when, as a result of its defeat in the First World War, the territory was transferred to British control and became Tanganyika.

The colonial period

Further legislation in 1873 had made the slave trade illegal, the slave market in Zanzibar was closed and the Protestant cathedral erected on the site. But slavery lingered on. The trade was illegal, but the institution of slavery existed openly until Britain took over the mainland from the Germans in 1918, and covertly, it is argued, for many years thereafter. Many former slaves found that their conditions had changed little. They were now employed as labourers at low wage rates in the clove plantations. Zanzibar continued to prosper with the expansion of trade in cloves and other spices. The fine buildings that make Zanzibar Stone Town such a glorious place were constructed by wealthy Arab slavers and clove traders, British administrators and prosperous Indian businessmen and professionals. These structures were so soundly built that they have survived for the most part without repairs, maintenance and redecoration from 1964 to the present.

The wealth of the successive Sultans was considerable. They built palaces in the Stone Town and around Zanzibar Island. Islamic law allowed them to have up to four wives, and their wealth enabled them to exercise this privilege and raise numerous children. Until 1911 it was the practice of the Sultan to maintain a harem of around 100 concubines, with attendant eunuchs. The routine was established whereby the Sultan slept with five concubines a night, in strict rotation. The concubines had children, and these were supported by the Sultan.

Social practices changed with the succession of Khalifa bin Harab, at the age of 32, as Sultan in 1911. He was to reign until his death, in 1960, at the age of 81. The harem and concubines were discontinued – apart from anything else, this proved a sensible economy measure. Gradual political reforms were introduced and the practice of Islam was tolerant and relaxed. Social pressures on non-Muslims were minimal. But the office of the Sultan was held in considerable awe. As the Sultan drove each day to spend the afternoon a few kilometres away at his palace on the shore, his subjects would prostrate themselves as he passed. In 1959, when it was suggested that there should be elected members of the Legislative Councils, and Ministers appointed to deal with day-to-day matters of state, the Sultan received numerous delegations saying change was unnecessary and the Sultan should retain absolute power. The present Sultan is still addressed as 'Your Highness' when Zanzibaris visit him.

David Reed, writing for *Readers' Digest* in 1962, described Zanzibar as the "laziest place on earth – once a Zanzibari has caught a couple of fish, he quits for the day, to retire to his bed, or the heavenly chatter of the coffee house". He developed his theme – "Once a clove has been planted, its lethargic owner has only to sit in the shade and watch as its tiny green buds grow into handsome pounds sterling. Even when the market is in the doldrums, a good tree may produce as much as £6 worth of cloves a year for its owner. In better times, it simply rains money on those who sleep below."

Despite these impressions of tropical torpor under a benevolent ruler, however, there were significant tensions. Several small Arab Associations combined to form the Zanzibar

National Party (ZNP) in 1955. The leader was Sheikh Ali Muhsin, educated at Makerere University in Uganda with a degree in agriculture. The leadership of the party was Arab, and their main objective was to press for independence from the British without delay. Two African associations, active with small landless farmers and agricultural labourers, formed the Afro-Shirazi Party (ASP) in 1957. The leader was Sheikh Abeid Karume, at one time a school teacher, a popular and charismatic personality, with great humorous skills that he exercised to the full at public meetings.

Although the ZNP tried to embrace all races, the fact was that they were seen as an Arab party, while the ASP represented African interests. Arabs comprised 20% of the population, Africans over 75%. Elections to the Legislative Council in 1955 were organized on the basis of communal rolls – that is, so many seats were allocated to Arabs, so many to Africans, and so on. This infuriated the ZNP who wanted a common electoral roll so that they could contest all seats. They boycotted the Legislative Council. When a ZNP member broke ranks, he was assassinated, and an Arab was executed for his murder. The next elections, in 1957, were held on the basis of a common roll, and the ZNP did not win a single one of the six seats that were contested. ASP took five and the Muslim League one. More damaging, Ali Muhsin insisted on a head-to-head with Karume in the Ngambo constituency, and was soundly beaten, polling less than 25% of the votes cast. ZNP's belief that they could draw broad-based support was very badly dented. In the next four years, the ZNP greatly increased its efforts with youth and women's organizations, and published five daily papers. It was also felt that wealthy Arab landowners and employers flexed their economic muscles to encourage support for ZNP among Africans. ZNP was greatly assisted in 1959 by a split in the ASP. Sheikh Muhammed Shamte, a Shirazi veterinary surgeon with a large clove plantation in Pemba, formed the Zanzibar and Pemba People's Party (ZPPP). Two other ASP members of the Legislative Council joined Shamte, and the ASP was left in a minority with just two seats.

In the run-up to Independence, there were three more elections. In the first, in January 1961, ASP won 10 seats, ZNP took nine and ZPPP was successful in three. A farce ensued in which both ASP and ZNP wooed the three ZPPP members. One supported ASP and the remaining two supported ZNP, creating a deadlock with 11 apiece. In the event, ZNP and ASP formed a coalition caretaker government on the understanding that new elections be held as soon as possible.

For the June 1961 elections a new constituency was created, to make a total of 23 seats. ASP and ZNP won 10 each, and ZPPP three. However, ZPPP had committed itself to support ZNP, and this coalition duly formed a government. However, ASP had gained a majority of the popular vote (albeit narrowly at 50.6%) and this caused resentment. The improved performance of ZNP in the two elections after the debacle of 1957 was bewildering to ASP. There were serious outbreaks of violence, and these were clearly along racial lines and directed against Arabs. There were 68 deaths of which 64 were Arab.

In 1962 a Constitutional Conference was held at Lancaster House in London, attended by the main figures of the three political parties. A framework was duly thrashed out and agreed, with the Sultan as the constitutional Head of State. The number of seats was increased to 31 and women were given the vote. Elections in 1963 saw ASP gain 13 seats, ZNP 12 and ZPPP six. A ZNP/ZPPP coalition government was formed under the leadership of Muhammed Shamte of ZPPP. Once again ASP had the majority of the popular vote with 54%. Independence was set for later that year, on 10 December.

The old Sultan had died in 1960 and was succeeded by his son Abdullah bin Khalifa, who was to reign for less than three years, dying of cancer in July 1963. His son, Jamshid Bin Abdullah, became Sultan at the age of 34.

The revolution

It has been described as 'the most unnecessary revolution in history'. At 0300 on the night of 12 January 1964, a motley group of Africans, armed with clubs, pangas (long implements with bent, curved blades, swished from side to side to cut grass), car springs, bows and arrows, converged on the Police Headquarters at Ziwani on the edge of Zanzibar Stone Town. There were two sentries on duty. John Okello (see box, page) was the leader of the attacking force. He rushed forward, grappled with one of the sentries, seized his rifle and bayonetted him. The other sentry was hit by an iron-tipped arrow. Encouraged, the attackers stormed the building. In a matter of moments the police had fled, and the mob broke into the armoury. Thus armed, they moved on to support other attacks that had been planned to take place simultaneously at other key installations – the radio station, the army barracks, and the gaol. By midday, most of the town was in the hands of Okello's forces.

As the skirmishes raged through the narrow cobbled streets of the historic Stone Town, the Sultan, his family and entourage (about 50 in all) were advised to flee by the Prime Minister and his Cabinet. Two government boats were at anchor off-shore. The Sultan's party was ferried to one of these, and it set off to the northwest to Mombasa, in nearby Kenya. The government there, having gained Independence itself only a month earlier, had no desire to get involved by acting in a way that might be interpreted as hostile by whatever body eventually took control on the island. The Sultan was refused permission to land, and the boat returned southwards down the coast to Dar es Salaam in Tanganyika. From there the party was flown to Manchester and exile in Britain.

Okello began the business of government by proclaiming himself Field-Marshal, Leader of the Revolutionary Government, and Minister of Defence and Broadcasting. Members of the ASP were allocated other ministries, with Abeid Karume as Prime Minister. Meanwhile there was considerable mayhem throughout the islands, as old scores were settled and the African and Arab communities took revenge upon one another. Initial figures suggest that 12,000 Arabs and 1000 Africans were killed before the violence ran its course.

A trickle of countries, mostly newly independent African states and Soviet regimes recognized the Karume regime fairly promptly. In February 1964 Karume expelled the British High Commissioner and the Acting US Chargé d'Affaires as their countries had not recognized his government.

Army mutinies in Kenya, Tanganyika and Uganda earlier in the year, the presence of British troops in the region and some ominous remarks by the US Ambassador in Nairobi about Communist threats to the mainland from Zanzibar all served to make Karume anxious. He felt vulnerable with no army he could count on, and what he saw as hostile developments all around. He needed some support to secure his position.

On 23 April, Karume and Julius Nyerere signed an Act of Union between Zanzibar and Tanganyika to form Tanzania. Later the mainland political party merged with ASP to form Chama Cha Mapinduzi (CCM), the only legal political party in Tanzania.

The union

The relationship between Zanzibar and the mainland is a mess. It is neither a proper federation nor a unitary state. Zanzibar retains its own President (up to 1995, *ex officio* one of the Vice-Presidents of the Union). It has a full set of ministries, its own Assembly, and keeps its own foreign exchange earnings. Mainlanders need a passport to go to Zanzibar, and cannot own property there. No such restrictions apply to Zanzibaris on the mainland. Despite comprising less than 5% of Tanzania's total population, Zanzibar has 30% of the aseats in the Union Assembly. The practice of rotating the Union Presidency between Zanzibar and the mainland meant that from 1985-1995 two of the occupants of the top three posts (the President and one of the two Vice-Presidents) come from Zanzibar. Zanzibar has not paid for electricity supplied by the mainland for over 15 years.

Despite all these privileges (which annoy the daylights out of many mainlanders) the Zanzibaris feel they have had a rough time since 1964. The socialist development strategy pursued by Tanzania after 1967 has seen living standards fall in Zanzibar. Where once the inhabitants of Zanzibar Town were noticeably better off than the urban dwellers in mainland Dar es Salaam, they now feel themselves decidedly poorer. They consider that if they had been able to utilize their historical and cultural links with oil-rich Oman they would have benefited from substantial investment and development assistance.

The legitimacy of the Act of Union has been called into question – it was a deal between two leaders (one of whom had come to power unconstitutionally) without any of the democratic consultation such a radical step might reasonably require. Separatist movements have emerged, pamphleting sporadically from exile in Oman and Scandinavia, and suppressed by the Tanzanian government. A Chief Minister in Zanzibar, Seif Sharrif Hamad, was dismissed when it was thought he harboured separatist sympathies. Later he was detained for over two years on a charge of retaining confidential government documents at his home.

Sharrif Hamad was the candidate for the Zanzibar Presidency of the Civic United Front (CUF), an already registered party. Support for CUF in the islands prior to the election was very strong but, victorious by a only narrow margin in both the Presidential and Assembly elections, a recount was called, and the incumbent Salim Amour was declared President with 50.2% of the vote (Hamad had 49.8%). CUF and Hamad were incensed at the outcome, and CUF briefly boycotted the Zanzibar Assembly. Political turmoil and outbreaks of violence followed, but CCM kept its position as poll winner. The CCM won further elections in 2000, and again violence flared amid accusations of fraud. Many CUF supporters fled to Kenya after deadly clashes with police. Both parties signed a reconciliation agreement in 2001. Under the ruling pro-union CCM, Zanzibar is set to remain part of Tanzania. But the CUF, which enjoys strong support on Pemba, has called for greater autonomy; some CUF members have called for independence. In 2005, the political status quo was maintained with CCM winning the elections with a majority, but there was anger, particularly on Pemba – a stronghold of the CUF party – caused by the belief that the results had been rigged. The next elections will be held in December 2010. Because of the possibility of violence on Zanzibar and Pemba during elections, you are ill advised to visit during these times.

Stone Town

It may not have a particularly romantic name, but Stone Town is the old city and cultural heart of Zanzibar, where little has changed for hundreds of years. It's a delightfully romantic place of narrow alleys, crumbling mosques, and grand Arab houses with giant brass-studded wooden doors. Most of the buildings were built by the Omani sultans in the 19th century when Zanzibar was one of the most important trading centres in the Indian Ocean. European influences such as balconies and verandas were added some years later. The walls of the houses are made from coralline rock, which is a good building material, but erodes easily. Many of Stone Town's 1900 historical houses have crumbled beyond repair, whilst others have been beautifully renovated. Since Stone Town was deservedly declared a World Heritage Site by UNESCO in 2000, the Stone Town Conservation Authority is working towards restoring the ancient town before these buildings are lost for ever. Most hotel accommodation is in the restored old houses and rooms are decorated with antiques, Persian rugs and the delightful four poster Zanzibarian beds. At least two nights is warranted in Stone Town to soak up the atmosphere, take one or more of the interesting half or full day tours on offer to sights in and around the city, and to learn a little about its fascinating history.

Ins and outs → *See also Ins and outs, page 56.*

Getting there If arriving at the airport, which is 6 km from town, you will be badgered by the many taxi drivers. Ask inside the airport what you should pay for a taxi to take you the short distance into town, which will help with bargaining once outside. A taxi should cost in the region of US$10-15, or alternatively there are buses and *dala-dala* to town for less than US$1. There is a bureau de change in the airport. Some of the more upmarket hotels and resorts offer free airport pick ups, so it always worthwhile asking.

The ferry terminal is in the Malindi area of Stone Town. Many of the hotels are within walking distance of the ferry terminal, or alternatively you can take a taxi directly from the port. The booking offices for the ferries are clustered around the jetty where you will need to reconfirm the date of your return ticket to Dar if you have not already done so when booking the ticket. The dhow harbour is next to the port, but remember it is illegal for foreigners to travel between the mainland and the islands by dhow. → *For further details, see Transport, page 85.*

Safety
Safety is becoming an increasing concern on Zanzibar. There have been violent robberies, at knifepoint, of tourists even during daylight hours in Stone Town and its environs. There is speculation that the perpetrators are mainland Tanzanians, as Zanzibaris are usually noted for their honesty. Be careful walking after dark, especially in poorly lit areas. Avoid alleyways at night, particularly by the Big Tree on Mizingani Road and the Malindi area near the port. Valuables can usually be left in your hotel safe as an extra precaution. At night use taxis to get back to the hotel, which can be found easily around the major restaurants and nightclubs. Exert caution on quiet beaches. Ignore anyone that might offer you drugs on the street. Drug use is illegal and the police may be watching the drug pushers – you will get into all sorts of serious trouble if caught negotiating with them. Quite surprisingly, there is a growing problem of heroin use amongst some young Zanzibaris and there is a concern about how and by whom the drug made its way on to the island. It is not uncommon for travellers in hire cars or motorcycles to be stopped by the police while driving to one of the beaches. The police may try to claim that your papers are not in order – basically they are looking for a small bribe. If you ask for a receipt or suggest that you want to go to the actual police station to pay the fine, they will wave you through.

Sights

The area west of Creek Road is the original Stone Town and a tour of it will take at least a day. But it is such a fascinating place that you could easily spend a week wandering the narrow streets and still find charming and interesting new places.

Creek Road
A good place to start a walking tour is from the **Central Darajani Market** on Creek Road. This was opened in 1904 and remains a bustling, colourful and aromatic place. Here you will see Zanzibarian life carrying on as it has done for so many years – lively, busy and noisy. Outside are long, neat rows of bicycles carefully locked and guarded by their minder while people are buying and selling inside the market. Fruit, vegetables, meat and

② Stone Town

N

100 metres
100 yards

Sleeping 🛏

236 Hurumzi & Tower Top
  Restaurant **10** *C4*
Abuso Inn **2** *D2*
Africa House **1** *D2*
Al Johari **16** *D2*
Beit-al-Amaan **3** *E3*
Beyt al Chai **21** *D1*
Chavda **6** *D3*
Clove **7** *C4*
Coco de Mer **8** *D3*
Dhow Palace **9** *D2*
Flamingo Guest
  House **11** *E4*
Florida Guest House **12** *E4*
Garden Lodge **13** *E3*
Haven Guest House **14** *E3*
Karibu Inn **17** *D2*
Karibu Zanzibar **29** *D2*
Kiponda **18** *C4*
Malindi Guest House **20** *A6*
Marine **22** *A5*
Mazson's **23** *D2*
Pyramid Guesthouse **26** *B5*
Shangani **30** *D2*
St Monica's Hostel **27** *D5*
Tembo House **31** *D2*
Zanzibar House **33** *D3*
Zanzibar Palace **37** *C4*
Zanzibar Serena Inn **36** *D1*
Zenji **38** *A5*

Eating 🍴

Archipelago **9** *C2*
Baobab Tree **2** *D4*
Dolphin **7** *D2*
Forodhani Gardens **6** *C2*
Kidude Café **19** *C4*
La Fenice **5** *D2*
Le Spices
  Rendez-vous **10** *E2*
Livingstone's **4** *C2*
Luis Yoghurt Parlour **11** *D3*
Mercury's **1** *B4*
Monsoon **3** *C2*
Old Fort **18** *C3*
Pagoda **13** *D2*
Sea View Indian **17** *B4*

Bars & clubs 🍸

Dharma Lounge **8** *E4*
Starehe **12** *D1*

To Dar es Salaam & Pemba

New Dock

Mizingani Rd

KIPONDA

Beit-al-Sahel
(People's Palace) **18**
Nyumbaya Moto St

FORODHANI

Aga Khan Mosque

Hurumzi St

Changa Bazaar

Jamituri
(Forodhani)
Gardens **6**

Orphanage **3**

Old
Fort **18**

Zanzibar
Dive Centre-
One Ocean

Mambo
Msiige **4**
31

Bahari
Divers **9**

Air
Tanzania

Upendo
Means Love

Shangani St

Zanzibar
Gallery

17 **2**
11

Bohora
Mosque

Hamamni
Persian Baths

St Joseph's
Catholic Cathedral

Coastal Air

Ras Shangani

36

21

16 29

SHANGANI

30

Tippu Tip's
House

Mathews
House

5

Barclay's

Suicide Alley

23

Kenyatta Rd

7

BAGHANI

Baghani St

6

Pipalwadi St

Sokomuhogo St

Former
English
Club

1

13

9

33

14

Zanzibar
Medical
Group

10

Kenyatta Rd

13

VUGA

8

Vuga Rd

3

12

National Library
& High Court

Zanzibar Channel

People's
Gardens
(Victoria
Gardens)

State
House

National
Museum

To Airport

① ② ③ ④

The Big
Tree

Iju
Mos

Gu
Ai

fish are all for sale here as well as household implements, many of them locally made, clothing and footwear. On Wednesday and Saturday there is also a flea market selling antiques and bric-a-brac. Note that the chicken, fish and meat areas are not for the squeamish – the smell and flies can be somewhat overwhelming.

Returning to Creek Road, after a further 200 m there is a large crossroads. To the left, a dual carriageway leads up to the 1960s developments of Michenzani – ugly concrete flats built by the East Germans during Tanzania's socialist period. To the right is New Mkunazini Road, and after about 50 m another right leads into the cathedral courtyard. The building to the left of the entrance to the courtyard is the **Anglican Missionary Hospital**, which is constructed on top of the old slave chambers. The **Anglican Cathedral**, was built in 1887 on the site of the old slave market to commemorate the end of the slave trade. You can pick up guides here who will for a small fee give you a short tour of the slave chambers and cathedral (daily 0800-1800). The altar is on the actual site of the slave market's whipping post. The marble columns at the west end were put in upside down, while the bishop was on leave in the UK. Other points of interest are the stained-glass window dedicated to David Livingstone who was instrumental in the abolition of the slave trade, and the small wooden crucifix said to have been made from the wood of the tree under which Livingstone died in Chitambo in Zambia. If you can, try to go up the staircase of the cathedral to the top of the tower from where you will get an excellent view of the town. There are services in Swahili every Sunday, and in English once a month. Also on Creek Road is the **City Hall**, a wonderfully ornate building that has recently been restored.

Sensitivity to Zanzibar culture

Zanzibar has a relaxed and sympathetic attitude to visitors. However, the islands are predominantly Muslim and as such Zanzibaris feel uncomfortable with some Western dress styles. In the towns and villages it is courteous for women to dress modestly, covering the upper arms and body, with dress or skirt hemlines below the knee. Wearing bikinis, cropped tops, vests that reveal bra straps, or shorts causes offence. For men there is no restriction beyond what is considered decent in the West, but walking around the towns bare-chested or with no shoes is considered offensive. Zanzibaris are either very vocal in expressing their offence, or by contrast are too polite to say anything. It is because of the latter that many tourists continue to take this advice unheeded. When on the beach it is acceptable to wear swimwear, but if a fisherman or harvester wanders by, it is polite to cover up. Some tourists sunbathe topless on the beaches – this is hugely insensitive and completely inappropriate. It is worthwhile remembering that whilst you may see other tourists wandering around in inappropriate dress, this doesn't mean that you should do the same. Behave like a responsible tourist and cover up. Other sensitivities to consider are during the holy month of Ramadan when most Muslims fast during daylight hours. It is considered the height of bad manners to eat, drink or smoke in the street or public places at this time. Although alcohol is freely available, drunken behaviour is not regarded with tolerance and is considered offensive by most non-drinking Muslims. Finally, public displays of affection are also considered to be inappropriate.

Western tip

The People's Gardens on Kaunda Road, also known as the Victoria Gardens, were originally laid out by Sultan Barghash for the use of his extensive harem. The grand pavilion was renovated in 1996 by German aid agencies. Many of the plants in the garden were added in the 1880s by naturalist and British Resident Sir John Kirk. Opposite the gardens and behind a white wall is the **State House**. Originally built as the British Residency, it was designed to complement the earlier Arabic buildings such as the People's Palace. Since independence the building has housed the President's Office. Note that photography is not permitted around the State House.

Mathews House is close to **Africa House Hotel**, just to the south of Ras Shangani at the western tip of the town. Before the First World War it was the residence, with characteristic overhanging balconies, of Lloyd Mathews (1850-1901). Mathews was a naval officer who was put in charge of the Sultan's army in 1877 (he was a mere Lieutenant of 27 at the time). Later he became Chief Minister and was known as the 'Strong Man of Zanzibar'. The **Africa House Hotel** is on Suicide Alley and was once the English Club, opened in 1888 (the oldest such club in East Africa), see box, page . One of the great events at the English Club used to be the New Year's Eve fancy dress ball, when great crowds of dumfounded Zanzibaris would gather to stare at the crazy *wazungu* (whites) in their costumes. It has been beautifully restored to its former glory and the upstairs terrace bar is one of the best places in Zanzibar for a drink at sunset (see also Sleeping, page 74). A little further down Suicide Alley is **Tippu Tip's House**, named after the wealthy 19th-century slave-trader, which has a splendid carved wooden door and black and white marble steps. Tippu Tip was the most notorious of all slavers and Livingstone's arch-enemy – the latter's report of the massacre at Nyangwe, in the Congo, where Tippu Tip had commercial hegemony, led ultimately to the abolition of the slave trade.

Also at the western tip of the town is the building known now as **Mambo Msiige**, which was built in 1847 and was once owned by a slave trader. It is said that he used to bury slaves alive within the walls of the building and added many thousands of eggs to the mortar to enhance the colour. Since then the building has been used as the headquarters of the Universities Mission to Central Africa and later as the British Consulate.

Old Fort

The Old Fort (also known as the Arab Fort or *Ngome Kongwe*) is in the west of the town next to the House of Wonders (see below). This huge structure was built in 1700 on the site of a Portuguese church, the remains of which can be seen incorporated into the fabric of the internal walls. Its tall walls are topped by castellated battlements. The fort was built by Omani Arabs to defend attacks from the Portuguese, who had occupied Zanzibar for almost two centuries. During the 19th century the fort was used as a prison and in the early 20th century it was used as a depot of the railway that ran from Stone Town to Bububu. It is possible to reach the top of the battlements on the west side and look at the towers. The central area is now used as an open air theatre, with a traditional music and dance show on Tuesdays, Thursdays and Saturdays at 1930. The fort also houses an art gallery, several small shops selling crafts and spices, plus a tourist information desk. There is also a charming café, with tables in the shade of a couple of large trees.

On the south side of the fort you can take a walk down Gizenga Street (used to be Portuguese Street) with its busy bazaars. This will lead you to **St Joseph's Catholic Cathedral**, designed by Henri Espérandieu, who designed the Basilica in Marseille and loosely based this work on it. The cathedral is well used and holds regular Mass. When not in use, the doors may be closed, in which case entrance can be gained by the back door, through the adjoining convent. On the opposite side of the road is the **Bohora Mosque**.

Beit-el-Ajaib (House of Wonders)

Close to the fort and opposite the Jamituri Gardens, this is Zanzibar's tallest building. It has four storeys surrounded by verandas and was built in 1883 by a British marine engineer for Sultan Barghash and served as his palace. The name 'House of Wonders' came about because it was the first building on the island to have electricity and even a lift. It has fine examples of door carving. At the entrance are two Portuguese cannons, which date from about the 16th century. In 1896 in an attempt to persuade the Sultan to abdicate, the palace was subjected to a bombardment by the British navy. Inside, the floors are of marble and there are various decorations that were imported from Europe; there are also exhibits from the struggle for independence. The building once served as the local headquarters of Tanzania's political party CCM, but was fully restored in 2002 as the **Museum of History and Culture** ⓘ *Mon-Sat 0900-1800, US$3*, with several permanent exhibitions on the history of the Swahili Coast.

Jamituri (or Forodhani) Gardens

The formal gardens are in front of the House of Wonders and the Old Fort and were once the location for the port's customs sheds before the port was moved in 1936 to the deepwater anchorage. Complete with a bandstand, the gardens are a pleasant place to stroll and watch the young boys diving off the sea wall but since 2008, the gardens have been closed for renovation and their re-opening has been postponed several times. In the meantime, the food stalls of the **Forodhani Market** have been moved to the streets near the Old Fort and sheets of corrugated steel surround the site. The market sells an extraordinary variety of snacks and seafood cooked on charcoal burners under paraffin lamps. Kebabs, freshly squeezed sugar-cane milkshakes, grilled calamari and prawns, omelettes, chips, pieces of fried fish, mussels, crab claws – everything is quite delicious and very cheap. At the time of writing, it remains to be seen whether the renovated gardens will retain their original charm or whether the area might be somewhat 'sanitized'.

Adjacent to the Jamituri Gardens is Zanzibar's **Orphanage**, which has previously been an English Club and an Indian School. The road here passes through a tunnel and if you follow it, the second building on the right has a plaque on the wall that reads: "This building was the British Consulate from 1841 to 1874. Here at different times lived Burton, Speke, Grant and Kirk. David Livingstone lived here and in this house his body rested on its long journey home." If the tide is low enough it is possible to pass down the side of the British Consulate and onto the beach, from where the magnificent houses can be viewed to their best advantage. Today, this building houses **Livingstone's Bar and Restaurant**, another good sundowner location with tables on the beach.

Beit al-Sahel (People's Palace)
① *Tue-Sat 1000-1800. US$3.*
The palace on Mizingani Road, north of the House of Wonders, is where the sultans and their families lived from the 1880s until their rule was finally overturned by the revolution of 1964. It was built in the late 1890s for members of the Sultan's family and for his harem. Following the revolution in 1964 it was renamed the People's Palace and was used by various political factions until it was turned into a museum in 1994. There are three floors of exhibits and it is well worth a visit. There is a wide variety of furniture including the Sultan's huge bed. Look out for the formica wardrobe with handles missing – obviously very fashionable at the time. There are good views from the top floor. The palace has grounds that can sometimes be viewed, containing the tombs of Sultan Seyyid Said and his two sons Khaled and Barghash. Heading north from the People's Palace is the **Big Tree**, which was planted in 1911 by Sultan Khalifa. Today it shelters local dhow builders.

Na Sur Nurmohamed Dispensary
Often called the 'Old Dispensary', this very ornate building is on Mizingani Road, north of the Big Tree. It was built in 1887 by Thaira Thopen, Zanzibar's richest man at the time, to commemorate Queen Victoria's Silver Jubilee. It's one of the most imposing of Stone Town's buildings, with four grand storeys and wrap-around decorative balconies. It served as a dispensary in colonial times and was one of the first buildings to be successfully restored to its former glory and today is the **Stone Town Conservation and Development Corporation**. Inside is a small tourist development known as the Zanzibar Cultural Centre with fixed priced shops, including a jeweller, curio and clothes boutique and a small, very pleasant cheap restaurant with a shady courtyard.

Port and dhow harbour

Further up Mizingani Road is the main port and the dhow harbour, which is a lively and bustling part of the Malindi quarter. The deepwater harbour has wharfs piled high with containers, and the landing is most frequently used by boats and hydrofoils from Dar es Salaam and Pemba. Built in 1925, the port remains essentially the 'industrial' end of town, with docks, cargo sheds and a clove distillery. The dhow harbour is at its busiest in the morning when the dhows arrive and unload their catches, and buyers bargain and haggle over the prices. These days very few dhows cross the Indian Ocean, unlike times gone by when fleets would arrive carrying goods from Arabia and the Orient, returning loaded with slaves, ivory and the produce of the islands' plantations. The best time to see one of these large ocean-going dhows is between December and March, before they return on the south-westerly monsoon. There is still plenty of smaller dhow traffic all year round between Zanzibar and the mainland, most bringing building materials and flour to Zanzibar.

Livingstone House

On Malawi Road, Livingstone's House was built around 1860 for Sultan Majid. It was also used by many missionaries and explorers as a starting point for expeditions into deepest, darkest Africa. Most notably, David Livingstone lived here before beginning his last journey to the mainland in 1866. Since then, it's been a laboratory (among other things) for research into clove production. It is now home to the Zanzibar Tourism Corporation.

Hammani Persian Baths

In the centre of Stone Town on Hammani Street, these baths were built by Sultan Barghash in 1888 for use as public baths and have been declared a protected monument. The building of the baths was overseen by a specialist team from Persia. If you want to look inside, ask for the caretaker who will show you around for a small fee (US$0.50). There is no water any more, so you have to use your imagination to imagine it in its heyday.

National Museum

ⓘ *Creek Rd, south end of town. Mon-Sat 0900-1800. US$3 for both buildings.*

The museum is in two buildings and although fairly run down and shabby has some interesting exhibits relating to Zanzibar's history. It was built in 1925 and has relics and exhibits from the sultans, the slave traders and European explorers and missionaries. Livingstone's medicine chest is here and the story of the German battleship the *Königsberg*, sunk during the First World War in the Rufiji Delta, is documented. There are also displays of local arts and crafts. If you are 'out of season' for the Spice Tour, it has an interesting exhibition on clove production. There is a giant tortoise in the grounds of the natural history museum and library next door and a door here, near the junction of Creek Road with Nyerere and Kuanda Roads, is reputedly one of the oldest doors on the island.

Around Stone Town

Changuu Island

ⓘ *You can get there through one of the tour agencies on a half day tour for about US$30, but it is just as easy – and cheaper – to find a boat yourself. Many boats will take you across to the island, and come back at a prearranged time to pick you up for about US$10 per person.*

Ask around on the beaches in front of the Sea View Indian Restaurant or Tembo Hotel. Just ensure that you only pay when you have been safely deposited back on the mainland. There is also a US$4 landing fee on the island.

Also known as **Prison Island**, Changuu Island is almost 5 km northwest of Stone Town. It was once owned by an Arab who used it for 'rebellious' slaves. Some years later in 1893 it was sold to General Mathews, a Briton who converted it into a prison. However, it has never actually been used as such and was later converted to serve as a quarantine station in colonial times. The prison is still relatively intact and a few remains of the hospital can be seen including the rusting boilers of the laundry. There is good snorkelling, windsurfing and sailing from the beautiful little beach, though jellyfish can sometimes be a problem. The island is also home to giant tortoises, which are supposed to have been brought over from Aldabra (an atoll off the Seychelles) around the turn of the 20th century. They stand up to a rather staggering 1 m high and could feasibly be hundreds of years old. The tortoises are no longer roaming freely over the island because many were stolen. Now they are kept in a large fenced area. You can buy leaves to feed the tortoises. The **Changuu Island Resort** is a simple and reasonable café serving cold beers and basic meals like grilled fish and salad and also rents out snorkelling gear.

Chapwani Island

Also known as **Grave Island**, Chapwani Island is a nearby private island with one exclusive lodge on it (see page 78). There is an interesting cemetery with headstones of British sailors and marines who lost their lives in the fight against slavery and in the First World War. The island itself is 1 km long and 100 m wide with a perfect swath of beach on the northern edge. The forested section is home to a number of birds, duikers and a population of colobus monkeys (how they got here is a bit of a mystery).

Kiungani, Mbweni and Chukwani

① *To the south of town off the airport road near the Mbweni Ruins Hotel.*

The route south of Stone Town will take you past Kiungani where there was once a hostel built in 1864 by Bishop Tozer for released slave boys. A little further on are the ruins of the **Mbweni Settlement**, which was also established for rescued slaves. This was built in 1871 by the Universities Mission to Central Africa. In 1882 St John's Church was built in the same place for the use of the released slaves. There is a fine carved door and a tower. Also at Mbweni is **Kirk House**, which was built by Seyyid Barghash in 1872. Kirk came to Zanzibar as the Medical Officer as part of Livingstone's expedition to the Zambezi. He played an important role in the fight to end the slave trade and in 1873 was appointed His Majesty's Agent and Consul General in Zanzibar. He was also a botanist, introducing to the island a number of plants said to have originated from Kew Gardens, including cinnamon, vanilla, mahogany and eucalyptus. Further south at Chukwani are the **Mbweni Palace Ruins**. This was once a holiday resort of Sultan Seyyid Barghash and it had a wonderful position overlooking the sea. However, it has been totally neglected and as a result is slowly crumbling away. The main palace has completely disappeared, although some of the other buildings do remain and may be toured.

Chumbe Island

① *The island is a private conservation project and has an all-inclusive resort of the same* *name (see page 78). A day trip can be booked directly with the park, T024-223 1040, www.chumbeisland.com, or through **Mbweni Ruins Hotel**, US$80 per person including transport, snorkelling equipment, nature trail guides and a buffet lunch. Note that they only take day guests if they're not fully booked with overnight visitors – it's best to make enquiries in advance.*

Approximately 4 km offshore southwest from the Mbweni Palace ruins lies the **Chumbe Island Coral Park**. This is an important marine park with a wonderful reef of coral gardens that can be viewed from glass-bottomed boats. The reef remains in a pristine state and is shallow (between 1-3 m according to tides). If you swim up to the reef ridge it's possible to spot shoals of barracuda or dolphins.

There are nearly 400 species of fish here: groupers, angelfish, butterfly fish, triggerfish, boxfish, sweetlips, unicornfish, trumpetfish, lionfish, moorish idols, to name but a few. The snorkelling opportunities are excellent but scuba-diving is not permitted in the park. There are nature trails through the forest on the island, the home of the rare roseate tern and coconut crab, the largest land crab in the world that can weigh up to 4 kg, and it is now a refuge for the shy Ader's duiker, introduced to the island with the assistance of the World Wide Fund for Nature. There is also an old mosque, and a lighthouse built in 1904.

Stone Town listings

For Sleeping and Eating price codes and other relevant information, see pages 12-17.

⊜ Sleeping

Accommodation on Zanzibar ranges from town hotels to beach resorts, and from local-style, budget accommodation to 5-star luxury. The decor and furnishings in most are traditional Zanzibar, with antiques and ornate Zanzibari 4-poster beds. Bookings can be made directly through the hotel, or through tour operators. Check that the VAT is included in the quoted prices on the hotel tariff. Reservations for the peak seasons (Jul-Sep and Nov-Jan) should be made well in advance. Note that there is often a surcharge over the Christmas and New Year period. At most places children under 18 years get substantial discounts. Most beach resorts offer bungalow-type accommodation and watersports like diving and snorkelling. Some of these are all inclusive, while others offer the option of B&B, half board or full board rates. Note that camping is not permitted on Zanzibar. As with elsewhere in Tanzania, room rates are quoted in US$, though the smaller budget hotels will often accept TSh. Credit cards are now accepted by all the larger hotels and resorts. If you have not pre-booked accommodation in Stone Town, you need to walk around and find a hotel that suits. Young men will tout for business, offering hotels, taxis, spice or other tours. They will usually pounce on you as soon as you get off the ferry. Some can be very aggressive and persistent. A polite 'no thank you' is rarely a successful method to rid yourself of their services. If you have just arrived you could tell the touts that you have already booked hotel accommodation from Dar es Salaam, and if you make your own way to a hotel insist that the management give no commission to any touts who may be following. Other strategies for tout evasion include saying you have been on all the tours, and that you are leaving tomorrow and have already bought the ferry ticket. It is better to deal directly with one of the many tour companies for excursions and organize everything in the confines of their office.

Stone Town *p64, map p66*

\$\$\$\$ Beyt al Chai, Kelele Square, opposite **Serena Inn**, T0774-444111 (mob), www.stonetowninn.com. Closed during May. This beautiful hotel takes its name from its previous occupation as a tea house and has just 6 exotically and individually decorated rooms with 4-poster Zanzibari beds, silks and organza fabrics in an opulent Arabian style. Breakfast is served in the pretty courtyard and the restaurant is highly recommended (see Eating, page 79). Doubles start at US$155 with breakfast.

\$\$\$\$ Zanzibar Palace Hotel, Kiponda, T024-223 2230, www.zanzibarpalacehotel.com. Another beautiful boutique hotel with all 9 rooms individually furnished in stunning Arabian styles. The rooms even have DVD players and there's a DVD library in the lobby. Tea and coffee is served in the bedrooms before breakfast and some of the rooms have huge stone baths as their centre-piece. It's worth checking the website to choose a room before booking because they are all so different. The restaurant has a daily and à la carte menu and pre-ordering is preferred. Set menu of 5 courses US$37, 3 courses US$28.

\$\$\$\$ Zanzibar Serena Inn, Shangani St, Shangani Sq, direct lodge number T024-223 3587, www.serenahotels.com. One of the best hotels in East Africa and a member of Small Luxury Hotels of the World. Stunning restoration of 2 historic buildings in Stone Town funded by the Aga Khan Fund for Culture. A seafront hotel with 51 luxury rooms and 10 suites and a swimming pool. Beautifully decorated with antique clocks, Persian rugs, carved staircases, chandeliers and brass-studded doors. The several restaurants have excellent but pricey menus. Wonderful location with first-class service.

\$\$\$ 236 Hurumzi, behind the House of Wonders, T0777-423266 (mob), www.236 hurumzi.com. 236 Hurumzi is the new name for the **Emerson and Green Hotel**, now that Emerson has moved on to other ventures. (His new hotel, **Emerson Spice** in the Kiponda area is completed but remains closed at the time of writing, with no indication of an opening date). Beautiful, individually themed rooms in restored 19th-century house with old Zanzibari furniture and fittings, original stucco decor, ornate carved doors and stone baths, lower rooms have a/c. All rooms have a bottle of water and fresh jasmine flowers are scattered on the pillows at bedtime. 2006 saw the opening of a new block of 6 rooms, following the same individual styles as the original ones but larger and slightly more expensive. There is also an apartment next door at 240 Hurumzi where the 6 bedrooms are let out individually and are particularly good value. The highlight here is the spectacular open-sided rooftop restaurant **Tower Top** – no shoes, sit on cushions, not cheap but worthwhile – a really magical experience. This is the second tallest building in Stone Town so the views over the rooftops are quite spectacular.

\$\$\$ Africa House Hotel, just off Kenyatta Rd, on Suicide Alley, T0774-432340 (mob), www.theafricahouse-zanzibar.com. This used to be the English Club in the pre-independence days and in 2001 was completely restored to its former glory. The hotel is now under new management. The building has many arch-ways, studded wooden doors, cool stone floors, 2 restaurants and a wide rooftop terrace with a bar which is *the* place on Zanzibar to sit and watch the sunset, sundowner in hand (although there have been reports of slow service). There are 15 elegantly decorated rooms with a/c, TV and Wi-Fi. Tastefully furnished throughout with antiques, original photographs and paintings by local artists, and the library houses a rare collection of many first editions and antiquarian books. Considerable discounts on room rates during low season (Apr-Jun).

$$$ Al Johari, 116 Shangani, T024-223 6779, www.al-johari.com. A brand new boutique hotel, which opened in Jan 2009. A lovely wooden turning staircase leads to the 15 rooms on 3 floors, all decorated in a very contemporary style with flat-screen TVs, minibars, a/c, and some with jacuzzi baths and double sinks in the bathrooms. The rooftop lounge and bar have great dual-aspect views of Stone Town and the ocean, and a waterfall feature that runs all the way down to the ground floor. Good reports of the food here at their Zanzibar Fusion restaurant, live Taarab music on Sat. Reports welcome.

$$$ Chavda, in the heart of Stone Town, off Kenyatta Rd, T024-223 2115, www.chavda hotel.co.tz. A good mid-range establish-ment in a large restored Arab mansion with 40 large rooms, comfortable and well decorated, if slightly inauthentic. Reasonable restaurant serving international and Chinese food and a good rooftop bar, both open to non-guests.

$$$ Dhow Palace Hotel, just off Kenyatta Rd, T024-223 0304, www.dhowpalace-hotel.com/ dhowpalace.html. Substantially extended 4 years ago, there's an attractive pool in a lovely interior courtyard between the old and new wings, with a bar selling snacks and soft drinks. Large rooms with high beamed ceilings, lovely bathrooms, a/c variable effect, fans, fridge, phone and antique furniture. Central courtyard and a very good rooftop restaurant that is rarely busy.

$$$ Tembo House Hotel, Forodhani St, T024-223 3005, www.tembohotel.com. This is a beautifully restored historic building that was the American Consulate in the 19th century. Rooms are decorated with antique furniture and have a/c, satellite TV, and balconies overlooking either the ocean or swimming pool courtyard. Great location on the beach, the food is good, and the staff are very friendly and willing to negotiate over rates. Excellent value. Recommended.

$$$ Zanzibar House Hotel, at the back of the **Dhow Palace Hotel**, off Kenyatta Rd, T0774-432340 (mob), www.zanzibarhotel.co.tz.15 rooms along similar lines to those in**Africa House Hotel**, its sister hotel and the place guests here go to for their restaurant and bar – it's a 5 min walk – since there are no facilities. There is a spa here though, and a huge lawned garden for guests to relax in. Doubles US$160.

$$ Abuso Inn, Shangani, opposite **Tembo House Hotel**, T0777-425565 (mob), abusoinn@gmail.com. The 22 en suite rooms here are spacious and spotless, with lovely wood flooring and furniture, a/c, mosquito nets and fans. Reception is on the first floor. Rates US$75 for a double including breakfast.

$$ Beit-al-Amaan, Vuga Rd, opposite Victoria Gardens, T024-223 9366. As an alternative to staying in a hotel, this private apartment with a large salon and 6 rooms can be booked for a group or each individual room can be let out, suitable for groups of 2-11 people. Very nicely furnished, each of the rooms have private bathrooms, and there's also shared kitchen with fridge and microwave and large living room. Breakfast is included in the room rate and is served to all the guests in the salon. Friendly and excellent value from US$79 for a double.

$$ Clove, Hurumzi St, behind the House of Wonders, T0777-484567 (mob), www.zanz ibarhotel.nl. A good mid-range option, run by Lisette, a Dutch lady. It's in a nice quiet square with an excellent roof bar and restaurant with free Wi-Fi access for residents and a great sea view. The building itself is quite modern by Stone Town standards, but the interiors have been remodelled to include elements of the more traditional Zanzibari style. Rooms have fridge, fan and en suite bathrooms with hot water. Don't take bookings for single nights.

$$ Hotel Marine, Malawi Rd, Malindi, diagonally across from port entrance, T024-223 2088, hotelmarine@africaonline.co.tz.

Zanzibar doors

At last count, there were 560 original carved doors in Zanzibar. When a house was built the door was traditionally the first part to be erected, and the rest of the house built around it. The tradition itself originates from the countries around the Persian Gulf and spread through Afghanistan to Punjab in India where they were reported in the first half of the 12th century. They started to feature in Zanzibar houses in the 15th century, but most of those surviving today were built in the 18-19th centuries. The greater the wealth and social position of the owner of the house, the larger and more elaborately carved his front door. The door was the badge of rank and a matter of great honour amongst merchant society. British explorer Richard Burton remarked in 1872: "the higher the tenement, the bigger the gateway, the heavier the padlock and the huger the iron studs which nail the door of heavy timber, the greater the owner's dignity".

Set in a square frame, the door is a double door opening inwards that can be bolted from the inside and locked from the outside by a chain and padlock. Popular motifs in the carvings on the doors include the frankincense tree that denotes wealth, and the date palm denoting abundance. Some of them feature brass knockers, and many are studded with brass spikes. This may be a modification of the Indian practice of studding doors with sharp spikes of iron to prevent them being battered in by war elephants. In AD 915, an Arab traveller recorded that Zanzibar island abounded in elephants, and in 1295 Marco Polo wrote that it had 'elephants in plenty'. These days there are no elephants, and the studs are there merely for decoration. The doors are maintained by the Stone Town Conservation and Development Corporation who keep a photographic record, and a watchful eye that they are not removed and exported.

3-star establishment near the gates of the main harbour. Comfortable rooms have a/c, satellite TV and en suite bathrooms and are decorated with traditional Zanzibari furniture. The restaurant serves local, Indian and Chinese dishes and there's room service. Note that this is a busy area and the street noise can be obtrusive. Be wary around the port area at night.

$$ Mazson's Hotel, Kenyatta Rd, Shangani, T024-223 3694, www.mazsonshotel.net. 35 rooms with a/c, fridge, TV, rooftop restaurant, in a whitewashed 19th-century building with wraparound balconies, and gardens with a fountain. Being renovated at the time of our visit – reports welcome.

$$ Shangani Hotel, Kenyatta Rd, across from the Old Post Office, T024-223 3688, www.shanganihotel.com. Clean and straightforward rooms with a/c, TV, fridge, fans, mosquito nets, own bathrooms and balconies overlooking the old town. There are nicer places to stay in this price range – with more polite managers – but the location is central and convenient and they have an internet café next door. Double bed and breakfast is US$75.

$$ Zenji Hotel, Malindi, opposite Cine Afrique building, T0776-705592 (mob), www.zenjihotel.com. Owned by a Zanzibari/Dutch couple, this small hotel near the port is very community focused, with all local furniture and crafts, locally sourced food and Zanzibari staff. It has 9 individual rooms very reasonably priced from US$50 including breakfast, served in the rooftop restaurant. Very good reports and helpful, friendly staff.

$ Coco de Mer Hotel, between Shangani St and Gizenga St, 1 block east of Kenyatta Rd,

T024-223 0852, cocodemer_znz@yahoo.com. This is a popular backpackers' choice with 13 basic rooms with bathrooms, fans and mosquito nets and some have TVs. Has a good restaurant (See Eating, page 80) and bar and it's in a central location. Clean and friendly, double rooms are about US$50.

$ Flamingo Guest House, Mkunazini St, just north of junction with Sokomuhogo St, not far from Vuga Rd, T024-223 2850, flamingo guesthouse@hotmail.com. Very good value at around US$10-15 per person. Simple, most rooms with shared showers, a small book exchange and satellite TV in the lobby.

$ Florida Guest House, off Vuga Rd, T024-223 3136, floridaznz@yahoo.com. Has been recommended by some readers, another simple budget guesthouse but in a noisy location, communal showers, twin rooms, the ones upstairs are quieter and nicer, and 1 room has 4 beds with a/c and TV, that is ideal for a group of friends travelling together.

$ Garden Lodge, Kaunda Rd, in Vuga opposite the National Library/High Court, T024-223 3298, gardenlodge@zanlink.com. Lovely gardens, peaceful and quiet with friendly staff. The rooms are basic and a bit tired but cheap. There is a combination of twins, triples and a 5-bed dorm, with bathrooms. Rates US$40 for a double.

$ The Haven Guest House, off Vuga Rd, T024-223 5677/8, thehavenguest@ hotmail.com. Secure budget place to stay. Rooms with or without bathrooms, plenty of hot water, mosquito nets and fans. Breakfast included in the price, self-catering kitchen, spotlessly clean and very friendly, owned by Mr Hamed.

$ Hotel Kiponda, Nyumba ya Moto St, behind the People's Palace, T024-223 3052, www.kiponda.com. Another nicely restored building with simple clean rooms, mosquito nets, some rooms are self-contained, others have spotless shared bathrooms. Central location with sea views, fans. Good value but look at the rooms before deciding as

they vary in size. Breakfast is served in the rooftop restaurant but no other meals are available.

$ Karibu Inn, next to **Coco de Mer Hotel**, T024-2233058, karibuinnhotel@zanzinet.com. Very popular and deservedly so, one of the best locations in Stone Town, tucked away behind the Old Fort. 25 rooms all with bathrooms, a/c is US$10 extra, fans, double rooms have fridges, also dorms for about US$15 per person, pre-booking is advised as it is frequently used by large overland groups. Excellent management who are very helpful and can organize all activities.

$ Karibu Zanzibar, Shangani, next door to **Al Johari**, not to be confused with **Karibu Inn** next to **Coco de Mer Hotel**, T024-223 0932, magoma.52@hotmail.com. This is a straight-forward guesthouse with 9 small but spotless rooms, all gleaming new and with their own bathrooms, nets, fan, a/c and TV. US$50 for a double with breakfast.

$ Malindi Guest House, Funguni Bazaar, Malindi St, T024-223 0165, www.zanzibar hotels.net/malindi. Excellent value place with a wonderful atmosphere. Central courtyard with plants, plenty of space to relax, clean, prices include breakfast. There's a rooftop coffee shop and bar with views of the harbour and the fisherman landing their catch every morning. Some of the rooms have bathrooms whilst others are dormitories with shared facilities. The only downside is that Malindi is not the safest part of Stone Town after dark – exercise caution if coming home late at night.

$ Pyramid Guesthouse, Kokoni St, behind the Ijumaa Mosque near the seafront, T024-223 3000, pyramidhotel@yahoo.com. Charming staff, modest accommodation, a mixture of self-contained rooms and dorms for as little as US$10 per person. The rooms vary in size so ask to see a few, simple but recommended. Breakfast is served on the roof and they offer free pick up from the port or airport.

$ St Monica's Hostel, New Mkunazini St, T024-223 0773, secactznz@zanlink.com. An old building next to the Anglican Cathedral with very clean and comfortable but simple rooms with or without bathrooms, mosquito nets and balconies. Price includes breakfast. Has a restaurant next door.

Around Stone Town p71
$$$$ Chapwani Private Island, reservations, Italy, T+39 (0)51-234974, www.chapwaniisland.com. This is an exclusive private island about 10 mins from Stone Town by speed boat, offering super-luxury and privacy in only 10 rooms in 5 bandas right on the beach in reed chalets with 4-poster beds. At night there are fantastic views of Stone Town. Seafood is the main feature on the restaurant menu, activities include volley ball, canoeing, and snorkelling. Prices are in the region of US$160 per person half board.

$$$$ Chumbe Island Coral Park, T024-223 1040, www.chumbeisland.com. This is a special place to stay. The utmost care has been taken to minimize the environmental impact of this resort; sustainably harvested local materials were used in the construction of the 7 luxury cottages and dining area, there is solar power and composting toilets, and rainwater is collected as the source of fresh water. Recognition of these efforts has been given through various awards and nominations over recent years. The emphasis is very much on the wildlife, coral reefs and ecology of the island and a stay here makes for an interesting alternative to the other beach resorts. Excellent food. Rates from US$250 per person, including all meals and soft drinks, boat transfers, snorkelling trip and forest trail.

$$$ Mbweni Ruins Hotel, south of Stone Town, T024-223 5478/9, www.adventure camps.co.tz. Built in the spacious grounds of the ruins of the first Anglican Christian missionary settlement in East Africa.

Private beach, pool, garden setting, open-air restaurant under thatch, art gallery, 13 suites with a/c and fans, 4-poster beds, mosquito nets, balconies, free shuttles to Stone Town 5 times a day. Organizes various tours around the island.

$$ Zanzibar Ocean View, 10-min walk from Stone Town along Nyerere Rd, close to the beach, T024-223 3882, www.amaan bungalows.com. This newly refurbished hotel on the beachfront at Kilimani is the closest beach resort to Stone Town. Rooms are comfortable and clean with nets, own bathrooms and sea view. Restaurant and bar, and they can arrange all the usual tours and transfers.

❷ Eating

Stone Town p64, map p66
There are a few moderate standard eating places in Zanzibar, many of them serving good, fresh seafood, and you will not usually need to reserve a table. Since this is a Muslim society, not all of the restaurants serve alcohol and if a bottle of wine is an essential part of your dining pleasure, it's advisable to check whether this is available beforehand. Most of the hotels have good restaurants and bars, many of which are on rooftops, that are also open to non-guests. During Ramadan it is difficult to get meals in the day time, other than in tourist hotels. It is not easy to find shops that sell spirits, although there is one on Kenyatta Rd in the Shangani area, opposite the Old Post Office.

♈ Africa House Hotel, see Sleeping, above. As well as a bar on the terrace that's perfect for sundowners, there are 2 restaurants here. **Tradewinds** is the more formal of the 2 with very good gourmet cuisine as well as Swahili dishes and seafood, whilst the **Sunset Grill** has an outside terrace, fresh fish dishes and BBQ meat grills. The atmosphere is great although there have been reports of slow service.

♈ Baharia, Zanzibar Serena Inn, see Sleeping, above. An expensive à la carte restaurant with fantastic food and attentive service in one of the most beautiful of the restored buildings on Zanzibar. It's worth eating here for a treat even if you are not staying. It's very romantic and you need to dress up.

Beyt al Chai, see Sleeping, above. Popular up-market restaurant with a Zanzibari theme, carved wooden ceiling beams and brightly coloured cushions. Lunch menu includes avocado salad with smoked sailfish for US$7 and various baguettes for US$6, and there are local specialties like green banana soup and fresh seafood on the dinner menu.

Tower Top Restaurant, 236 Hurumzi, see Sleeping, above. Here you can eat in wonderful surroundings on the rooftop; if you are not staying here you need to book a day ahead as space on the roof is limited. Semi-fixed dinner menus with the emphasis on seafood, with one seating starting at 1900, then take all evening to enjoy the excellent food and the sumptuous setting.

Archipelago, Kenyatta Rd, opposite the National Bank of Commerce, T024-223 5668. Open daily for breakfast, lunch and dinner, traditional Swahili dishes, salads, burgers and daily specials. Good coffee and cakes. Outdoor terrace with modern furniture overlooking the harbour. No alcohol.

Kidude Café, 236 Hurumzi, on the ground floor, see Sleeping, above, T024-2232784. Named after the famous Taarab singer Bi Kidude, this is a good place for lunch with a selection of sandwiches and wraps, as well as more exotic choices like creole fishcakes for US$7 and delicious shrimps with passion fruit dressing for US$8. Dinner is also excellent and there's a good wine list, albeit expensive.

La Fenice, on seafront just around the corner from **Serena**, T0777-411868 (mob). Good lunch as well as a dinner, authentic continental and Swahili seafood dishes.

Le Spices Rendez-vous, Kenyatta Rd, near the High Court, T0777-410707 (mob). Tue-Sun. Formerly the **Maharaja Restaurant**, it still serves up excellent Indian meals, snacks and seafood. Recommended.

Livingstone's Restaurant, in the old British Consulate Building, on the seafront just down from Kenyatta Rd, T0773-271042 (mob). In a great location on the beach, with a varied menu of continental and Swahili dishes, salads and pastas. Lively and popular, with occasional bands and artwork on the walls that's for sale. If you want a table on the beach in the evenings, it's best to book ahead. Wi-Fi available.

Mercury's, Malindi, T024-223 3076. Named after Freddie, with an atmospheric wooden outdoor terrace overlooking the harbour, serves pizzas, pasta, seafood BBQ, Thai, Indian and Zanzibari food and cocktails with good service. Great place to watch soccer games on the beach but food is a little overpriced. Live bands occasionally.

Monsoon, between Forodhani Gardens and the Old Fort, T0777-410410 (mob). Deservedly popular restaurant full of Zanzibari atmosphere, cushions on the floor indoors and a lovely garden terrace outside. Great food and friendly service, with traditional Swahili cuisine including dishes like king fish in coconut sauce and ginger-marinated beef salad. Taarab music in the evenings.

The Old Fort Restaurant, inside the fort, T0754-278737 (mob). Nothing special but the only place to eat in the fort now that **Sweet Eazy** has closed. Burgers for US$6, pizzas for US$6-9, Swahili dishes and BBQs too. Expensive for what you get – you're probably paying for the location. Traditional music and dance show on Tue, Thu and Sat.

Pagoda, has relocated from Funguni to the Shangani area, and is now only a few paces away from **Africa House Hotel**, T024-223 4688. Has really excellent spicy Chinese cuisine, generous portions. Go for a beer at the hotel first to watch the sunset.

Sea View Indian Restaurant, Mizingani Rd, T024-223 7381. A splendid location overlooking the harbour. You can eat inside or out and there is a wide range of food on the menu including delicious and good value curries, freshly cooked to order, but nevertheless service can be slow, and if you want to sit on the balcony, book ahead.

Baobab Tree, New Mkunazini Rd, near the UMCA cathedral. Large thatched roof built around the trunk of a baobab tree, open-sided seating area beneath, some meals, snacks, juices, bar.

Coco de Mer, see Sleeping, above. A popular place with good quality food at low prices including chicken Kiev, pili pili crab, octopus in coconut sauce, chicken tikka and sandwiches all for around US$4.

Dolphin Restaurant, Kenyatta St, T024-2231987. Popular place selling mainly seafood. Nothing special but one of the cheapest places where you can sit down. A sandwich will cost you about US$2.

Forodhani Gardens (also known as **Jamituri**), between the fort and the sea. At the time of writing, the gardens were closed and the stalls were on the streets around the Old Fort, so the market's lacking its true charm. Vendors were hopeful of returning by the summer but the re-opening of the gardens has been postponed twice so far. When up and running, this is a lively, atmospheric place to eat and shouldn't be missed. Here you can get excellent meat or prawn kebabs, lobster, grilled calamari and fish, corn on the cob, cassava and curries all very cheaply. It is very popular with tourists who return night after night, and fun to wander around even if you don't feel hungry. If you're thirsty, try some fresh coconut milk or freshly squeezed sugar cane juice. The 'African Pizza' (*mantabali*) is also well worth a try. You may need to haggle over some of the prices, but you will still come away very full

and with change from US$10. Just ensure everything is cooked well and inspect it carefully in the dim light. If it's not ask the vendor to throw it back on the coals for a little longer Try to keep a tab of what you have, or pay as you go along – some of the vendors have been known to bump up the bill when it comes to settling up.

Cafés
Luis Yoghurt Parlour, Gizenga St, not far from **Africa House Hotel**, T0765-759579 (mob). Mon-Sat 1000-1400, 1800-2200. Closes for long periods in low season while the owner goes away.Very small place serving excellent local dishes including lassi, yoghurt drinks, milk shakes, fresh fruit juices, spice tea, and fabulous Italian ice cream.

Bars and clubs

Stone Town *p64, map p66*
Africa House Hotel, see Sleeping, page 74. The most popular bar in the town on a wide marble upstairs terrace which looks out across the ocean. The beers are cold and plentiful although rather expensive, and it is a good place to meet people. Get there early if you want to watch the sun set.

Dharma Lounge, Vuga Rd, T024-223 3626. A popular nightclub, open 2000 until the early hours. Modern hi-tec club with a large dance floor and good selection of music.

Livingstone's and **Mercury's** (see Eating, page 79) are slightly cheaper places than Africa House (see above) to watch the sun set, both with a wide range of cocktails, Savannah cider, beers and wines. They both have live bands playing occasionally and Mercury's is a great spot to watch the locals playing soccer on the beach – they have some very skilled players.

Starehe, next to the **Serena Inn**. Good reggae music especially on Sat nights. Very popular.

Stone Town *p64, map p66*
Feb Sauti za Busara Swahili Music and
Cultural Festival. Held annually during the
second weekend in Feb, the 4-day festival
attracts talent from all over East Africa with
performances in music, theatre and dance.
See Dhow Countries Musical Academy,
www.zanzibarmusic.org, or www.busara
music.org, T024-223 2423, for more
information. *Sauti za Busara* means 'songs of
wisdom' in Kiswahili, and this annual festival
of Swahili music attracts the best musicians
and performers in the region. Held in Stone
Town, there are concerts (mostly in the Old
Fort) of traditional music, from Swahili taarab
and *ngoma* to more contemporary genres
that mix African, Arab and Asian music.
Feb Eid al-Haj (also called Eid al-Adha or Eid
al-Kebir). The Islamic festival of the annual
pilgrimage, or haj, to Mecca. It is the second
major holiday of Islam and a 3-day festival
of feasting and celebration in all Muslim
communities in Tanzania. For Muslims, this
holiday is about sacrifice, faith, and honouring
the prophet Ibrahim. Along the Swahili Coast,
and the islands of Zanzibar, each family
sacrifices a goat or sheep; a third of the meat
is given to the poor, another third to family
and friends, and the final third is kept by the
family to be served in a lavish meal. Any
family members or friends who made the
pilgrimage to Mecca that year are welcomed
home with much rejoicing. During the night
there is live Swahili taraab music and much
rejoicing.
Jul Zanzibar International Film Festival
of the Dhow Countries, held every year
during the first 2 weeks of Jul, www.ziff.or.tz.
Celebrates and promotes the unique culture
that grew as a result of Indian Ocean trade
and the wooden sailing dhow. All nations
around the Indian Ocean known as the dhow
countries are included in the celebration.
Contemporary artists, musicians, cultural

troupes, photographers and film makers
are showcased and their work promoted,
discussed, awarded, and explored. The
highlight is the Zanzibar International Film
Festival; film screenings take place around
Stone Town in various historic landmarks.
During the festival, workshops, seminars,
conferences and a variety of cultural and
arts-related programmes are open to the
public, with specific forums to attract and
creatively empower women and children.
Zanzibar Cultural Festival, held annually,
directly after the Zanzibar International
Festival of the Dhow Countries,
www.ziff.or.tzis. Held throughout the
archipelago, many performers from around
Africa perform at the annual Zanzibar Cultural
Festival but the Swahili culture is mostly
represented. Zanzibari *taarab* music and
traditional dances are performed by a rich
ensemble of cultural troupes and there are
exhibits of arts and crafts. Street carnivals in
Stone Town, small fairs, and canoe races also
take place.
Nov/Dec Eid al-Fitr (in Kiswahili also called
'Idi' or 'Sikuku,' which means 'celebration'). The
Muslim holiday that signifies the end of the
holy month of Ramadan. It is without a doubt
the central holiday of Islam, and a major event
throughout Tanzania, but especially observed
on the coast and Zanzibar. Throughout
Ramadan, Muslim men and women fast from
sunrise to sunset, only taking meagre food and
drink after dark. The dates for Eid al-Fitr vary
according to the sighting of the new moon,
but as soon as it is observed the fasting ends
and 4 days of feasting and festivities begin.
Stone Town is the best place to witness this
celebration when the whole of the town takes
to the streets.

⊙ Shopping

Stone Town *p64, map p66*
Central Darajani Market on Creek Rd, sells
mainly fresh fruit and vegetables and meat.
However, the shops nearby sell *kikois* and

kangas (sarongs), wooden chests and other souvenirs. Also try the small shops in the Old Fort, one shop sells only locally hand-crafted wooden boxes, many made of fragrant rosewood.

Abeid Curio Shop, Cathedral St, opposite St Joseph's Cathedral, T024-223 3832. Sells old Zanzibari furniture, clocks, copper and brass.

Capital Art Studios, Kenyatta St. Sells wonderful black and white photographs of old Zanzibar as well as prints of the Masai and other Tanzanian people. These make great souvenirs and look particularly good when framed in heavy wood.

Masomo Bookshop near the Old Empire Cinema just behind the Central Market, T024-223 2652. Has a good range of books and also sells Tanzanian and Kenyan newspapers.

Memories of Zanzibar, opposite Shangani post office, T024-223 9377, www.memories-zanzibar.com. Another upmarket shop with quality souvenirs, jewellery, handbags, cloth, cushions and books.

Upendo means love, just off Gizenga St, near Karibu Inn, T0784-300812 (mob), www.upendomeanslove.com. A new shop which sells great clothes for women and children made from kangas and kikoi. It's all about empowering local women and all the proceeds go to running a sewing school and workshop where women are trained and employed.

The Zanzibar Gallery, Mercury House, Shangani, T024-223 2721, gallery@swahilicoast.com. Reputedly the former home of Freddie Mercury, this beautifully decorated shop boasts the most comprehensive range of books in Zanzibar; guidebooks, wildlife guides, coffee table books and the best of contemporary and historical fiction from the whole of Africa. The CD collection focuses on the best of Swahili music traditions such as taarab. Authentic artworks, antiques, fabrics and textiles from Zanzibar and mainland Africa, and clothes. It also sells excellent postcards taken by the owner's son. Accepts credit cards.

⚠ Activities and tours

Stone Town p64, map p66
In order to maximize your time in Zanzibar it is worth considering going on a tour. All the tour companies listed under Tour operators offer the following range of tours:

City tour
This includes most of the major sites of Stone Town, such as the market, national museum, cathedral, Beit al-Sahel and Hammani baths. If you are interested in the architecture, this is a good opportunity to learn more about the buildings. Half day, US$20-25.

Cruises
Sabran Jamiil is a traditional 36 ft jahazi (ocean going dhow) that has been fully restored and is decorated with Persian cushions, flowing cloth and storm lanterns. Each evening between 1700-1900 she sails along the coast of Stone Town and you can get on at either the Tembo Hotel or the Forodhani Gardens. The views of the city from the water at sunset are gorgeous. The price of US$40 includes drinks and snacks.

Safari Blue, T0777-423162 (mob), www. safariblue.net This daily cruise departs from Fumba to the southwest of Stone Town several kilometres beyond the airport; transfers can be arranged. A full day trip around sandbanks, small islands and coral reefs, includes use of top quality snorkelling equipment with guides and instructors, sodas, mineral water and beer, and a seafood lunch of grilled fish and lobster, fruit and coffee. Dolphins can be seen most of the time. US$80 per person.

Diving
Zanzibar is a great place to go diving. There are 2 recommended diving schools in Stone

Zanzibar dive sites

Pange Reef The first sandbank west of Stone Town with a maximum depth of 14 m. There is an enormous variety of coral and lots of tropical reef fish such as clown fish, parrot fish, moorish idol and many others. Pange reef is ideal for Open Water Diver courses, as it offers calm and shallow waters. This is also a good spot for night dives, where you may see cuttle fish, squid, crab and other nocturnal life.

Bawe Island Bawe has a reef stretching around it with a maximum depth of 18 m. Here you will find beautiful corals like acropora, staghorn, brain corals and a large variety of reef fish.

Wrecks Wreck diving for all levels: At 12 m *The Great Northern* (built 1870), a British steel cable-laying ship, which sank on New Year's Eve 1902. She has become a magnificent artificial reef and is home to a number of leaf fish, lionfish and morays. Parts of the ship can still be identified and some relics may still be found (though not taken). *The Great Northern* is an ideal wreck for the beginner diver as she is only 12 m below the surface and is also great for snorkelling. The 30 m wreck of the *Royal Navy Lighter*, is home to large schools of rainbow runners, trevally, sweepers, and sometimes reef sharks, best suited for experienced advanced divers. At 40 m a steam sand dredger, *The Penguin*, is only suitable for very experienced deep water divers. Here you can find huge numbers of barracuda, big stingrays and morays.

Murogo Reef Maximum depth 24 m, 25 mins from Stone Town by boat. Sloping reef wall with a huge variety of coral and fish. Turtle are often seen here and this is usually the preferred dive site for the Open Water Diver course.

Nyange Reef The largest of all reefs on the west coast of Zanzibar and containing several dive sites, all of which are unique. A new species of coral has recently been identified here and marine biologists believe it to be endemic to Nyange.

Boribu Reef One of the best dive sites off Zanzibar and huge barrel sponges, large moray eels, pelagic fish and large lobsters are all features of this dive. In season whale sharks pass through. The maximum depth is 30 m.

Leven Banks On the north coast, this site is popular with advanced divers as <R>it lies near the deep water of the Pemba Channel and is home to big shoals of jacks and trevally. Famous for remote 'holiday brochure style' beaches and colourful reefs, the east coast diving is the most talked about on Zanzibar.

Mnemba Island Reached from Nungwi or Matemwe also on the north coast, has a wide range of sites varying in depth with exciting marine life. Great <R>for snorkelling too. Pungu Wall, East Mnemba, is a recommended dive for experienced divers looking for sharks, rays and groupers. This site can only be dived in calm conditions.

Thanks to **Zanzibar Dive Centre-One Ocean**, www.zanzibaroneocean.com.

Town that both offer good value. It is worth noting that the best time for diving in Zanzibar is Feb-Apr and Aug-Nov.

Bahari Divers, next to the National Bank of Commerce on the corner of Shangani and Kenyatta road, T0777-484873 (mob), www.zanzibar-diving.com. Offer all PADI courses to instructor level and snorkelling using a motorized dhow, German owned. If you book on line there is a 10% discount.

PADI Open Water course US$400, single dives US$70, discounts for multiple dives, snorkelling trips with lunch US$30.

Zanzibar Dive Centre-One Ocean, bottom of Kenyatta Rd, on the seafront, T024-223 8374, www.zanzibaroneocean.com. Motorized dhows and custom-built dive boats go to several coral reefs. PADI certificate course US$450 for open-water diving, including PADI materials. If you have a scuba certificate, 1 dive including boat trip to the reef costs US$75 and 2 dives US$100, including all equipment hire and lunch. The inexperienced are offered 'fun dives' for US$125, which include 30 mins' instruction of the basics, plus a 12-m deep dive on a coral reef, snorkelling is US$30 a trip, safety highest priority, with fully trained dive masters/instructors. Recommended.

Dolphin tour

Humpback and bottlenose dolphins swim in pods off Kizimkazi Beach on the southwest of the island, and are not always easy to spot. A dolphin tour includes transport by minibus to Kizimkazi, and transfer to a boat at the beach, a route that easily allows for a visit of Jozani Forest (see page 103). Prices and the quality of the boats vary, and many of the small boats do not run to a timetable but wait to fill up, usually accommodating 6-8 tourists. Book this excursion through a tour operator rather than with the touts on the beachfront in Stone Town. From Stone Town, a half day trip is around US$50-60. Full day including the dolphins in the morning and Jozani Forest in the afternoon is about US$60-70, depending on how many are on the tour, whether you want a private tour, etc.

North and east coast tour

All operators offer transport to the north and east coast beaches, which can be combined with tours. For example, you can be picked up in Stone Town and taken to the east coast via the Jozani Forest (US$35, US$25 if you only go to Jozani and return to Stone Town, see page 103) where the rare red colobus monkey is found. On the way to the north coast, you have the option of combining a morning Spice Tour and perhaps a visit to the Mangapwani slave caves, and ending the tour by being transferred to the hotels in Nungwi.

Spice tour

For centuries Zanzibar's cloves, nutmeg, cinnamon, pepper and many other spices attracted traders across the Indian Ocean. The exotic spices and fruits are grown in the plantations around Stone Town and there's ample opportunity to dazzle the senses as you taste and smell them and guess what they are. This tour is highly recommended in during season, out of season you may get weary of looking at leaves that look very similar. Most tours are by *dala-dala*, the longer ones also include lunch. Guides give detailed descriptions of the various plants. The henna tree produces a dye from its crushed leaves used by women to elaborately decorate their hands and feet in delicate patterns. On the tour you'll have the opportunity to have a body part painted, but with quick-drying Indian ink instead (henna takes all day to dry). The tours last 4 hrs and are offered via various tour operators, Half day, around US$25; full day with additional visits to the slave caves and beach at Mangapwani, around US$30.

Tour operators

All these operators offer the tours listed above and others including: historical ruins and slave relics, Prison Island. Some are also able to arrange dhow sailing trips to the smaller islands, visits to Pemba, domestic flights, and car and motorbike hire. This is certainly not a comprehensive list, there are so many tour operators to choose from. Alternatively, you may be able to book all excursions through your hotel.

Classic Travels & Tours, Shangani, T024-223 8127, kassimabdalla@hotmail.com.

Discover Zanzibar, Chukwani Rd, T024-223 3889, www.discover-zanzibar.com.

Easy Travel & Tours, Malawi Rd, opposite Hotel Marine, T024-223 5372, www.easy travel.co.tz.

Eco Culture Tours, Hurumzi St, T024-223 0366, www.ecoculture-zanzibar.org.

Equator Tours and Safaris, Sokomohogo St, T024-233 3722, eqt@zanlink.com.

Exotic Tours and Safaris, 1st floor, Bombay Bazaar Building, Mlandenge, T024-223 63923, www.zanzibarexotictours.com.

Fisherman Tours and Travel, Vuga Rd, T024-223 8791/2, www.fishermantours.com.

Forodhani Car Hire, near Forodhani Gardens near the Old Fort, T0747-410186 (mob).

Furaha Tours, opposite La Fenice Restaurant, T024-223 2973, www.furahatours.com.

Links Tours and Travel, at the port, T024-223 1081, linktours@yahoo.com.

Marzouk Tours & Travel, opposite 236 Hurumzi, T024-223 8225, www.mtt-znz.com.

Mitu, T024-223 4636. Mr Mitu is one of Stone Town's most famous and formidable residents and has been running excellent Spice Tours in numerous languages for decades. He's now retired but guides he has trained run the show. They will take you on a tour visiting the Marahubi Palace, 2 spice plantations, the Kidichi Baths and a 1-hr trip to relax on the beach. They are good value. However, they have become very popular and you may find yourself in a large group of 30 or more. US$15 per person, including vegetarian lunch. Bookings are taken the evening before or from 0800 on the day, get there by 0900, depart 0930, return 1300-1600 (depending on whether or not you go to the beach).

Ocean Tours, opposite Zanzibar Serena Inn, T024-223 8280, www.oceantourszanzibar.com.

Sama Tours, Changa Bazaar St, T024-223 3543, www.samatours.com .

Simba Tours, T024-223 0687, www.simba tours.com.

Tanzania Adventure, Diplomat House, Mianzini, T024-223 2119, www.tanzania-adventure.com.

Tima Tours and Safaris, Mizingani Rd, T024-223 1298, tima@zitec.org.

Tropical Tours and Safaris, Kenyatta Rd, Shangani, T0777-413454 (mob), tropicalts@hotmail.com.

Zan Tours, Malindi St, T024-223 3116, www.zantours.com.

Around Stone Town p71

Zanzibar Heritage Conservation Park

An alternative to going on a Spice Tour is to visit this park in Jumbi, 12 km southeast of Stone Town. The park is a private enterprise, operated by the very knowledgeable Omar Suleiman, who will show you around the large garden of herbs, fruits and other plants, and also the small museum and aviary. A small entrance fee is charged, to get there ask a taxi driver to take you to Jumbi as the park is not widely known. There is a small sign on the left of the road as you approach the village.

⊖ Transport

Stone Town p64, map p66

You can arrange transfers by minivan through most tour agencies to get around the island. It will cost about US$10 per person to get to the beaches in the north or east. You can hire cars for about US$-50-60 per day, motorbikes for US$25-30 per day, and bicycles for US$5-10, from many of the tour operators. Sometimes they also charge a refundable deposit. Ensure all your paperwork is in order if driving.

Air

Several airlines have scheduled services to and from the mainland and Zanzibar airport.

Expect to pay in the region of US$81 one way. Some also operate a service between Zanzibar and **Pemba** which is around US$100 one way. The airline industry is highly changeable, so check times before travelling. **Air Tanzania** has flights to **Dar** daily at 0950 and 1700 (25 mins). These services connect with onward flights.

Precision Air has flights to **Dar** at 0830, 1150 and 1700 (20 mins) and there are connections to other domestic destinations from Dar. There are also daily direct flights between Zanzibar and **Nairobi** at 0730 (1 hr 45 mins); to **Arusha** at 1410, (1 hr 10 mins); and to **Mombasa**, Tue and Sat 1140, Thu and Fri 0915 (40 mins).

Coastal Air have daily flights to **Dar** at 0645, 0800, 0930, 1100, 1300, 1400, 1430, 1600 and 1715. The 1400 from Zanzibar continues to **Selous** and costs a further US$160 from Dar. There are also daily return flights to **Arusha**, which depart Zanzibar at 0930 and Arusha at 1215, take approximately 2 hrs and cost US$220 one way. There's a daily flight from Zanzibar to **Pemba** at 1430 (30 mins) that costs US$101.

Zan Air has scheduled daily flights to **Dar** at 0650, 1130, 1300, 1600 and 1730. To **Pemba**, 0945 and 1600. There is also 1 daily direct flight to **Arusha** at 1030.

Airline offices International airlines that serve Zanzibar are: **Emirates**, T024-223 4950, www.emirates.com. **Ethiopian Airlines**, T024-2231526, www.flyethiopian.com. **Gulf Air**, just off Malindi Rd towards the port, T024-223 2824. **Kenya Airways**, Kiponda, T024-223 2041, www.kenya-airways.com.

The domestic airlines that serve Zanzibar are: **Air Tanzania**, Shangani St, T024-223 0213, www.airtanzania.com. **Precision Air**, Dar, T022-213 0800, T022-212 1718, Zanzibar, Kiponda T024-223 4520, www.precisionair tz.com. **Coastal Air**, reservations, Dar, T022-

284 2700, Zanzibar Airport office T0713-670 815 (mob), www.coastal.cc. **Zan Air**, to the west of Malawi Rd, Malindi area, T024-223 3670, www.zanair.com.

Bus and dala-dala
Dala-dala, which are usually converted pickup vans with wooden benches in the back, and regular buses are the cheapest way of getting around the island. It will cost about US$2 to the east or north coasts, but they are hot, dusty and not very comfortable. Most go from the bus station on Creek Rd opposite the market. Buses with lettered codes serve routes in and around Stone Town. A to **Amani**, B to **Bububu**, and U to the **airport**, amongst others. Numbered vehicles go further afield, and tend to leave once a day around noon, returning early the next morning. Bus No 9 goes to **Paje**, **Jambiani** (3 hrs) and **Bwejuu** (4½ hrs), costing about US$4. Other buses from Creek Rd go to **Pwani Mchangani** and **Matemwe** (bus No 1), **Mangapwani** (bus No 2), **Fumba** (bus No 7), **Makunduchi** and **Kizimkazi** (bus No 10), **Nungwi** (bus No 16), and **Kiwengwa** (bus No 17). There is another bus station, Mwembe Ladu, 1 block north of the New Post Office about 1.5 km east of Stone Town. Bus No 6 from here goes to **Chakwa** (1½ hrs), **Uroa** and **Pongwe**.

Ferry
The booking offices of the ferry companies are on the approach road to the harbour. **Azam Marine**, T024-223 1655. **Flying Horse**, T0784-472497 (mob). **Sea Express**, T024-223 4690. **Sea Star**, T0707-223 3857 (mob). **Zanzibar Port's Corporation**, for general enquiries, T024-223 2857.

⊙ Directory

Stone Town *p64, map p66*
Banks There are ATM facilities at many of the banks in Zanzibar, including Barclay's near Maszon's Hotel, Shangani; **People's Bank**

of Zanzibar, T024-221 31118/9, behind the fort on Gizenga St, also has a branch at the Airport Terminal, T024-221 1189. **Barclay's**, ZSTC Building, Malawi Rd, Gulioni, T024-223 5796; **National Bank of Commerce (NBC)**, Shangani St, T024-223 31541. **Currency exchange** Banks often give an inferior rate compared with the foreign exchange (forex) bureaux, which are also open for longer hours. There are plenty of these all over Stone Town, just ensure you go into an office and do not deal with money changers on the street. **Immigration Director of Immigration**, T024-223 9148. If you lose your passport whilst on Zanzibar contact the immigration department who will arrange for an emergency travel document to get you back to Dar where the international embassies and high consulates are located. **Internet** There are many internet cafés all over Stone Town. Services are particularly good, with fast connections and reasonable prices. Expect to pay around US$1 for 1 hr. **Lost and stolen cards Visa and MasterCard Assistance Point**, next to Serena Inn,

Mon-Sat 0830-1730. You can withdraw cash against your credit card. **Medical** services **Mkunazini Hospital**, near the market, T024-223 0076, British trained doctor, pay fee to register, wait to see doctor then pay for any prescription necessary, pay again when you go to collect medicine: this may be at the clinic or in a nearby drug-store; **Zanzibar Medical & Diagnostic Centre**, near Majestic Cinema, off Vuga Rd, T024-223 3113; **Zanzibar Medical Group**, off Kenyatta Rd, T024-223 3134, 24 hr emergency number T0777-410954 (mob). **Money transfers Western Union** money transfer is available from the Tanzanian Postal Bank on Malawi Rd, Malindi area, T024-223 1798, open Mon-Sat 0830-1800. **Police** T024-223 0772. **Post office** The **New Post Office** is outside Stone Town, in Kijangwani, just over 1 km east of the Karume Monument, T024-223 1260. Bus A or M from the market will take you there. Poste restante are held there. **Old Post Office**, Kenyatta Rd, Shangani area, has a fax and they should be able to help with poste restante. **DHL**, opposite Serena Inn.

North to Nungwi

The stretch of coastline immediately to the north of Stone Town was once an area of villas, recreational beaches, and Sultans' out-of-town palaces. This is also the route that was once followed by the Bububu light railway and an iron pipeline that carried domestic water supplies to the town during the reign of Sultan Barghash. Today many of the ruined palaces can be visited, though little of their previous opulence remains and they are fairly overgrown. Nevertheless they offer an interesting excursion off the road to Nungwi. At the northern end of the island are the villages of Nungwi and Kendwa. Until recently these were sleepy fishing villages hosting a couple of backpacker's lodges, but today the two settlements are almost joined together by a ribbon of hotel development and this is one of the most popular spots on the island for a beach holiday. The party atmosphere along the Nungwi Strip may not appeal to everyone, but there is no denying that this is a wonderful stretch of palm lined beach. Days are warm and sunny, the Indian Ocean is a brilliant blue and the snorkelling and diving are excellent.

Maruhubi Palace ruins

The Maruhubi Palace ruins are about 3 km to the north of the town. They were built in 1882 by Sultan Barghash for his harem of what is said to be one wife and 99 concubines. The Palace was once one of the most impressive residences on the island. Built in the Arabic style, the main house had balustrade balconies, the great supporting columns for which can still be seen. From here you can imagine him looking out over his beautiful walled gardens, which are believed to have been inspired by the Sultan's 1875 visit to Richmond Park in London. An overhead aqueduct and lily-covered cisterns (or 'pleasure ponds') can also be seen on the site and are evidence of the extensive Persian Baths. On the beach are the remains of a fortified *seble* or reception area, where visiting dignitaries would have been welcomed. The palace was almost completely destroyed by a fire in 1899, the site is now very overgrown, and marble from the baths has long since been stolen.

Mtoni Palace ruins

Shortly after the Marahubi Palace, just before the small BP oil terminus, are the ruins of the earlier Mtoni Palace. Shortly before he relocated his court from Muscat to Zanzibar in 1840, Sultan Seyyid constructed the Royal Palace at Mtoni as his primary residence. The palace was abandoned by 1885, in favour of more modern residences built by Sultan Barghash (see Maruhubi Palace, above) and quickly fell into disrepair. Use as a storage depot in World War I caused further damage and now only the walls and part of the roof remain. The site, sadly, is sandwiched between commercial premises and the BP oil refinery.

Around 3 km North of Mtoni, to the left hand side of the road is **Kibweni Palace**. This fine whitewashed building is the only Sultan's Palace on the island to remain in public use, accommodating both the President and state visitors.

Persian Baths at Kidichi

ⓘ *1 km north of Kibwenii. Take a right hand turn opposite a small filling station, along a rough dirt road. Follow the track for 4 km out through the clove and coconut plantations.*

Built on the highest point of Zanzibar Island by Sultan Seyyid Said in 1850, they were for his wife who was the grand-daughter of the Shah of Persia, Fatah Ali, and are decorated in ornamental Persian stucco work. The remarkably preserved baths have a series of domed bathhouses with deep stone baths and massive seats. This is quite a contrast to the plain baths nearby at **Kizimbani**, which were built within Said's clove tree and coconut plantation. Persian poetry inscribed inside the baths at Kidichi has been translated (approximately) as "Pleasant is a flower-shaped wine/With mutton chops from game/Given from the hands of a flower-faced server/At the bank of a flowering stream of water". The beaches to the west of here are good and are the location of several resorts. **Fuji Beach** can be easily reached from Bububu Village, and is a great place to take a relaxing swim if you've been exploring the area. There is a disco on the beach every Friday. Any *dala-dala* with the letter B from the main road will get you to Fuji beach.

Mangapwani slave caves

ⓘ *If you want to get there independently, the caves can be reached by taking bus No 2 from Creek Rd opposite the market. It's best to take a torch.*

About 20 km north of Stone Town, these were used to hide slaves in the times when the slave trade was illegal but still carried on unofficially. One particular trader, Mohammed bin Nasser, built an underground chamber at Alwi that was used as well as the naturally formed cave. The cave itself is said to have been discovered when a young slave boy lost a goat that he was looking after. He followed its bleats, which led to the cave containing a freshwater stream (a blessing for the illegally confined slaves). You may well see women carrying water from this very same stream today.

Tumbatu Island

ⓘ *The White Sands Hotel in Kendwa organizes trips here.*

Northwest of Zanzibar, the island of Tumbatu is the third largest island in the archipelago and despite being only 8 km long by 3 km wide, it has a very individual history. The island contains Shirazi ruins of a large ancient town dating from the 12th century and about 40 of the stone houses remain. The Mvuleni ruins are in the north of the island and are the remnants of the Portuguese attempt to colonize Zanzibar. The island's people, the Watumbatu, are distinct from the people of Unguja. They speak their own dialect of Kiswahili and are fiercely independent, renowned for their aloofness and pride rather than their hospitality. They are strictly Muslim and generally do not welcome visitors to the island. They also have the reputation of being the best sailors on the East Coast of Africa.

Kendwa

South of Nungwi (see below), about 20 minutes walk (3 km) along the beach, is the small resort of Kendwa. It is reached by the same minibuses that transport visitors to Nungwi or by boat from Nungwi. The beach is especially known as a good place to swim (as is Nungwi) because the tide only retreats about 6 m at low tide, so swimming is possible at any time of day. A band of coral lies about 20 m off shore which offers interesting snorkelling, and trips can be organized by the hotels.

Nungwi

ⓘ *Tourist minibuses go from Stone Town throughout the day, take approximately 1 hr, and cost about US$10 each way, ask from any hotel or tour operator. There are also local dala-dala and the No 16 bus from Creek Rd also goes to Nungwi. These take about 2 hrs and cost about US$1 each way.*

At the north tip of the island is Nungwi, about 56 km from Zanzibar town. It's a pleasant fishing village surrounded by banana palms, mangroves and coconut trees, with a local population of around 5000. However, don't come to Nungwi expecting a quiet beach holiday – over recent years tourism has rapidly expanded in this area, large new resorts are going up at the time of writing, and Nungwi and nearby Kendwa Rocks have firmly established themselves as the party destination of the island. As well as resorts, there are a number of good beach-side bungalows, a short line of lively outdoor bars and restaurants known as the 'Nungwi Strip', and a few dive schools. The accommodation is of a good standard and most of Nungwi's cottages are built in a traditional African style with makuti thatched roofs to blend in with the natural surroundings. The bars are fantastically rustic and you'll find beautifully carved Zanzibari furniture sitting on the beach.

Down on the beach, you'll often see local men working in groups to build dhows or dhow fleets heading out to fish in the mid- afternoon. Boat building here has been a traditional skill for generations using historic tools and a 12-m boat takes approximately six months to build. Goats are slaughtered when certain milestones are reached (eg raising the mast) and verses and prayers are read from the Koran. Upon completion a big ceremony is organized and all the villagers are invited. Before the launch the boat builder hammers the boat three times in a naming ceremony.

The name of the village is derived from the Swahili word *mnara*, referring to the 70-ft lighthouse built here 1886 by Chance and Brothers. Currently it's in a restricted area, with access permitted only by special request and photography is prohibited. Nearby, there are two natural aquariums. **Mnarani Aquarium** ① *US$2.50,* was established in 1993 by a local resident in an attempt to help restore the local turtle population. Four varieties of turtle are endemic to Zanzibar; the hawksbill (*Ng'amba*); the green turtle (*Kasakasa*); the leatherback turtle (*Msumeno*) and the loggerhead turtle (*Mtumbi*). The aquarium has green turtles, which have a light grey/yellowish shell and hawksbill turtles, which have a yellowish/red shell. Their diet is seaweed and the hawksbill also eats fish. Any turtles hatched at the aquarium are released into the sea. Wild vervet monkeys live in the trees surrounding the rockpool.

You can buy basics at the small shops along the beachfront but it is much cheaper to go into the village where water, bread and other items are available. Remember to respect local custom if you go into the village. Women should cover their arms, shoulders and thighs. There are several places to check email in Nungwi at the resorts or at the small shopping centre on the Nungwi strip. However, the best place to get online is at the school; it's US$1 per hour but the proceeds go back into the school.

North to Nungwi listings

For Sleeping and Eating price codes and other relevant information, see pages 12-17.

🛏 Sleeping

North to Nungwi *p88*

$$$ Imani Beach Villa, Bububu Beach, T024-225 0050, www.imani.it. Only 7 clean, comfortable rooms with a/c, own bathrooms and traditional-style furniture. Breakfast is served in pleasant gardens that run down to the beach, other meals are a fusion of Mediterranean and African influences, with organic vegetables from their gardens. The quality and presentation of food is very high and you eat Swahili-style, seated on cushions around low tables. Restaurant open to non-residents. US$110 double B&B or US$700 for private use of the whole house for up to 14 people half board. Recommended.

$$$ Mtoni Marine Centre, between the ruined palace of Maruhubi and the Mtoni ruins to the north, 8 km from Stone Town, T024-225 0140, www.mtoni.com. Set in a large palm tree garden, the centre has a range of accommodation from shared bungalows to club rooms and suites. The Palm Garden apartments have private verandas, are traditionally furnished and have views of the beach. The bungalows have 1-3 bedrooms and are ideal for families. The restaurant is open air and has barbecue buffets and themed nights with live jazz or taarab music. There's also a beach cocktail and snack bar, a sports café, a spa and a sushi restaurant.

$$$ Salome's Garden, Fuji Beach, reservations through British agent, T+44 (0) 130 688 0770 www.africatravelresource.com. Lovely early 19th-century restored royal house surrounded by 7 ha of walled private orchards and tropical gardens running down to the beach full of bougainvillaea. Refurbished in 1997 as a luxury guesthouse or you can rent the whole house. There are 4 bedrooms sleeping a maximum of 10, with traditional Zanzibari 4-poster beds with mosquito nets, fans and beautiful antique decor.

$ Bububu Beach Guest House, Bububu Beach, T0777-422747 (mob), www.bububu-zanzibar.com. Rooms with en suite bathrooms, hot water, mosquito nets and fans. Laundry, fax and email available. Free shuttles to and from Stone Town on request. There's also a whole house that can be let out to a group of up to 8. The owner Omar Kilupi is a former chess master of Zanzibar and is always up for a game. Arranges transfers and tours.

$ Kibweni Beach Villa, 4 km north of Stone Town, T024-223 3496, www.geocities.com/kibwenibeach. Simple and friendly. Singles, doubles or triples (US$20/35/45), in a double story whitewashed building with tiled roof. Some rooms have sea views, all have a/c and en suite bathrooms. Restaurant serves local and oriental food. Can organize all tours.

Kendwa *p90*

$$ Kendwa Amaan Bungalows, T0777-411 141 (mob), www.kendwa.tanzania-adventure.com. 39 rooms in bungalows with mosquito nets, balconies, en suite bathrooms. Some set back on the hill and others on the beach. The restaurant is on the beach with tables in the sand and a cocktail bar. Lots of hammocks to lounge around in. Can arrange tours and offers free transfers to Nungwi.

$$ Kendwa Sunset Bungalows, T0777-413 818 (mob), www.sunsetkendwa.com. One of the better places to stay in Kendwa, with a choice of accommodation ranging from new apartment blocks to beach bandas – all are reasonably priced for what you get, perched on top of a small cliff above the beach. There is a very good bar and restaurant which does great fresh fish and pizzas. It has a slightly more organized feel to it, at least most of the time, with friendly staff. Dive centre on site.

$$ White Sands Hotel, T0777-417412 (mob), www.ajvtours.co.tz/whitesands. En suite bandas or bungalows on the hillside near the beach. A reasonably good restaurant specializing in seafood but lacking ambience. Can arrange diving and snorkelling.

$ Kendwa Rocks Hotel, T0774-415474 (mob), www.kendwarocks.com. This was the original backpackers' lodge at Kendwa and will appeal to people laid back enough not to worry about the variable levels of service and surly staff. Basic thatched bandas on the beach US$15 per person, or better quality bungalows for US$45 for a double. Fish, veggie and Indian food is available. Sometimes music pumps out late into the night, which may or may not be your thing – it's a popular place for 'full moon' parties. 24 hr Mermaid bar, Wi-Fi access available.

Nungwi *p90*

The price of a hotel room in Nungwi varies from US$20-500, so the resort appeals to all budgets. In recent years, new hotels, including large, soulless package resorts, have been built here and they effectively join up Nungwi with Kendwa to the south. If you want to avoid the crowds, the northwest of the peninsula is generally quieter and has some smaller, more intimate places to stay. The beach party crowds tend to hang out around the southern part of the village.

$$$$ Ras Nungwi Beach Hotel, T024-223 3767, www.rasnungwi.com. 32 rooms, some in the lodge, some beach chalets and 1 suite that is a huge detatched house with a plunge pool and total privacy from the rest of the hotel, costing US$900 a night. All rooms have ocean views, 4-poster beds, carved doors, en suite bathrooms, fans and balconies. The more expensive rooms have CD players and minibars. Restaurants and bars, pool, TV room and lounge areas under thatched roofs. There's a full range of watersports on offer, mountain bikes can be hired, excellent dive centre with good diving on the reef and deep-sea fishing. The hotel supports the local Nungwi Village community through the Labayka Development Fund, assisting with health and hygiene projects and schooling.

$$$$ The Z Hotel, on the west coast near **Amaan Bungalows**, T0732-940303 (mob), www.theZhotel.com. Opened in Jun 2008, Nungwi's newest hotel looks set to compete with **Ras Nungwi** as the best in the area. A boutique hotel with 35 elegant sea-view rooms boasting plasma TVs, Wi-Fi access and Phillip Starke furniture, it's a classy mix of Zanzibari and contemporary style. There's a relaxing infinity pool overlooking the beach and an open-air restaurant, serving African-continental fusion food, built up on stilts over the sea for more great views. The Cinnamon bar is also the perfect spot for sundowners. US$260 double room B&B.

$$$ Amaan Bungalows, T024-224 0026, www.amaanbungalows.com. Clean, self-contained rooms – the best are those with balconies right near the beach, although you pay more for this. 3 bars and a restaurant on site serve good quality food, and there's an internet café. Amaan is really the centre of the whole Nungwi strip and Fat Fish bar, with its thumping music is hugely popular, which means there is often a bit of a party scene. **Nungwi Travel**, who can organize tours, transfers and bicycle hire is based here.

$$$ Flame Tree Cottages, on the northwest side of Nungwi peninsula, T0777-479429 (mob), www.flametreecottages.com. Set in colourful gardens with coconut palms, frangi- pane and bougainvillea just off the beach, the 16 immaculate cottages are all named after trees or plants that are common to Zanzibar. All are en suite, with a/c, TV, fridge, net and fan, and are beautifully appointed with private verandas where guests are served breakfast. Some also have kitchenettes and self-catering can be arranged for a small surcharge. There's a candle-lit restaurant specializing in seafood and the whole place has an air of tranquillity about it. Rates are negotiable for longer stays.

$$$ Langi Langi, T0773-911000 (mob), www.langilangizanzibar.com. 34 rooms in bungalows just across the track from the beach; singles, doubles and triples, all with en suite bathrooms, hot water, a/c, fan, mosquito nets, veranda and hair dryer. The lounge area has satellite TV, telephone and fax, and there's a rooftop restaurant with reasonably priced food. Swimming pool, internet café, pleasant garden.

$$$ Mnarani Beach Cottages, near the lighthouse, a 20-min walk from the main strip, T024-224 0494, www.lighthousezanzibar.com. Ranges from simple cottages, to rooms in the main building, to family cottages, all with en suite bathrooms and Zanzibari beds. Friendly management, clean, comfortable and well maintained, great service and a good atmosphere. Discounts in low season. Near enough to Nungwi to enable you to visit the bars and restaurants, but far enough away to let you get a decent night's sleep afterwards. Breakfast included, full- and half-board available. Great seafront bar with hammocks, restaurant that focuses on seafood and international cuisine, laundry facilities, hot water, snorkelling, fishing and diving trips. Accepts major credit cards. Recommended.

$$$ Nungwi Village Beach Resort, www.nungwivillage.com. Beach cottages with thatched roofs, furnished with traditional- style Zanzibari wooden decor, en suite bathrooms, premium rooms have a/c. Bar, restaurant specializing in seafood, facilities for watersports including diving. Internet access, henna painting and massages also available.

$$$ Sazani Beach Hotel, near to **Ras Nungwi Beach Hotel**, T024-224 0014, www.sazanibeach.com. 10 en suite rooms, double or twin beds, veranda, electricity and fans, sea views. Tropical garden setting, quiet and well away from the 'strip'. The Pweza Juma bar and restaurant serves original dishes with local flavour, specializing in seafood and barbecues, morning tea brought to your room and buffet breakfasts are included in the price. There is a dive school on site offering PADI courses or snorkelling trips, and kitesurfing can be arranged.

Maviko ya Makumbi

As you walk along the beach you will see mounds of what look like stones, known locally as 'Heaps of Stones', but which are in fact deposits of coconut husks. Each Heap of Stones belongs to a family or sometimes an individual, and some are 60 years old, passed down from one generation to the next. They are made into coir and then used to make ropes, matting and decorations. The coconuts are buried in the mud for three to six months, which accelerates the decay of unwanted parts of the coconut, leaving the coir (the sea water helps to prevent insect infestation). The coir is then hammered to separate it out from the vegetable matter.

If you see a group of women working on the Maviko ya Makumbi, request permission before taking a photograph.

$$$ Smiles Beach Resort, just south of **Nungwi Village Beach Resort**, T0774-444334 (mob), www.smilesbeachresort.com. The 16 ensuite rooms are in 2-storey houses with wide spiral staircases to the upper floors. Each has ensuite, a/c and a TV, and their own terraces or balconies. There's a restaurant just off the beach (it doesn't serve alcohol).

$$ Paradise Beach Hotel, T0777-416308 (mob), shaabani_makame@hotmail.com. 18 rooms in a rather ugly, tired-looking block facing the sea, all with bathrooms and fans. The beach restaurant is popular with good quality food and a lively beach bar. **Zanzibar Watersports**, who are also based at Ras Nungwi, have recently opened here and offer PADI courses and snorkelling.

$ Baraka Bungalows, behind Paradise Beach, T0777-415569 (mob), http//barak bungalow.atspace.com. Has no direct sea frontage yet it is a beautiful little garden oasis with some of the best bungalows in this price range in Nungwi, simply furnished, all have own bathrooms and terraces, fans and nets, and some have a/c. US$45 for a double, includes breakfast, and there is a cheap restaurant with generous portions. There's also a sister guesthouse, **Baraka Annex** (same contact details), which is just opposite the entrance to Mnarani Beach Cottages on the northeastern side of the peninsula, and so about a 20-min walk from the main Nungwi drag. The 4 rooms here are more basic but cheaper at US$30 for a double with fans and nets and include breakfast. They also have a natural aquarium here, a massive rock pool with several turtles, the oldest and largest of which is 28 years – they plan to put him back into the sea to breed when he matures at 30.

$ Jambo Brothers Beach Bungalows, behind **East Africa Dive Centre** on the west side, T0777-492355 (mob), jambobungalows@yahoo.com. This is a bigger concern than its neighbours, **Union** and **Baraka Bungalows**, with 19 rooms set just back from the beach, 2 of which have a/c that bumps up the cost to US$80 – a lot for what you get. Otherwise, prices range from US$35-50 for a double for simple rooms with nets and fans, bathrooms and a small terrace outside. They have a restaurant and café selling soft drinks, and a beauty centre should you fancy a massage.

$ Romantic Bungalows, 2 mins' walk from the beach, set back behind **Flame Tree Cottages** and **Smiles**, T0732-940330 (mob), www.romanticbungalowszanzibar.com. Owned by the affable Eddy, this laid-back, friendly place is a good option for lower budgets, with 8 rooms in 4 bungalows set in secluded gardens. All rooms have their own bathroom, nets, fans and terraces, some have fridges. The gardens have hammocks and sunbeds scattered around, and there's a restaurant, satellite TV, internet and safe parking for vehicles. Dinner needs to be pre-ordered and it's soft drinks only, but there's a supermarket nearby where you can buy beer. Good value at US$40 for a double with breakfast, reductions in low season.

$ Union Beach Bungalows, on the west side of the peninsula, just north of **Baraka Bungalows**, T0777-876345 (mob), mrpoudi@ live.com. Low budget with 10 bungalows on the beach, each with their own bathrooms, nets and fans. Rates from US$35-60 for a double including breakfast.

⊛ Festivals and events

See page 81 for information on festivals which are held throughout the archipelago.

▲ Activities and tours

North to Nungwi *p88*
The beaches around Ras Nungwi are one of the few areas without a coral reef and you can swim at all tides here without walking out for miles to reach the sea, as is the case on the east coast.

A number of places organize 'sunset cruises' on dhows for US$15 per person.

Fishing
FishingZanzibar.com, Nungwi, T0773-387 5231 (mob), www.fishingzanzibar.com. Offers full- or half-day big game fishing trips to Levan Bank or Mnemba Island or longer live-aboard trips to Pemba Island. Rates start from US$500 for a half day for 6 fishermen.

Zanzibar Big Game Fishing, Ras Nungwi Beach Hotel, T0777-415660 (mob), www.zanzibarfishing.com. This is a similar operator to FishingZanzibar.com, and rates for a boat start from US$400 for a 5 hr trip.

Diving
Diving is good around Nungwi and Kendwa and several dive schools operate here. The recommended ones are: **Zanzibar Dive Centre-One Ocean Divers**, www.zanzibar oneocean.com, see page 84. They provide all equipment. Sorkelling equipment can also be hired from local shops.

Zanzibar Watersports, at Paradise Beach Hotel, www.zanzibarwatersports.com.

Kitesurfing
Nungwi has also become popular for kitesurfing, www.kitezanzibar.com.

To the northeast coast

The very northeast part of the island seems miles away from the party scene of the Nungwi area and has a more remote, 'get away from it all' feel. Villages like Matemwe stretch right up the coast, fringed with shady palms. The local people live a peaceful existence making a living from farming seaweed or octopus fishing. An extensive coral reef runs down the whole east coast of the island, protecting a long, idyllic white sandy beach that runs for miles and is one of Africa's most beautiful beaches. The only problem here is that the ocean is tidal, and during some parts of the day it's a very long walk over the tidal flats to reach the sea. Further south, particularly around Kiwengwa and Pongwe, there has been a mushrooming of fully inclusive resort properties along the coast, which are quite characterless and could quite frankly be anywhere in the world, many of them frequented by European package holiday makers. For the most part, it is necessary to book these through a tour operator in Stone Town, Dar es Salaam or Europe (many are Italian or Swiss owned) – or take a chance on getting a room when you arrive, although several do not take 'walk-in' guests. This is particularly risky in high season from June to September and over the Christmas and New Year period. There is very little choice of budget accommodation along the stretch of coast around Pongwe or Kiwengwa, although Matemwe has more options.

Ins and outs

Getting there Minibus transfers can be arranged in Stone Town and cost around US$15. Bus No 6 from the Mwembe Ladu station in Stone Town goes to Chwaka (1½ hours), and then continues north to Uroa and Pongwe. The No 17 bus from the Creek Road station in Stone Town also goes along the better part of the beach road as far north as Kiwengwa. Both cost approximately US$1.50.

Dunga Palace

Just over 20 km down the road from Stone Town are the ruins of the Dunga Palace, which was built by Chief Mwinyi Mkuu Ahmed bin Mohamed Hassan. Legend has it that during the palace's construction slaves were killed in order that their blood could be mixed with the mortar to bring strength and good fortune to the building. During the 1920s a nearby well was found to be 'half full of human bones'. King Muhammad died in 1865 and was succeeded by his son Ahmed, who died without an heir in 1873, ending forever the line of the Mwinyi Mkuu. Unfortunately, there is little left of the palace today beside bits of wall and arches, and the area has been taken over by a plantation.

Chwaka Bay

At the end of this road, 32 km from Stone Town via Dunga you will reach Chwaka Bay. On the way you will pass the small **Ufufuma Forest**, a home for Zanzibar red colobus monkey, Ader's duiker, impala and many bird species, and also the site of several caves. The forest has been actively conserved since 1995, and although not a very well-known attraction, tourists are welcome, with guided walks costing around US$5. Chwaka is a quiet fishing village overlooking a broad bay of shallow water and mangrove swamps. Its history is evident from a line of fine but decayed villas, standing above the shoreline on the coral ridge, and it was once popular as a holiday resort with slave traders and their families in the 19th century. There is a lively open-air fish market but little accommodation and most visitors head north along the coast to the hotels.

North of Chwaka

The road from Chwaka heads north through the coastal fishing villages where there are several accommodation options and watersports centres on what is a fantastic beach. **Uroa** is a lovely fishing village 10 km to the north of Chwaka, and is close to the Dongwe Channel, which offers suitable diving for novices. **Pongwe** is 5 km north of Uroa, and **Kiwengwa** another 10 km north of Pongwe, followed by **Pwani Mchangani**. From the main road between Kiwengwa and Pongwe, which is all tarmac now, there are sections where there seems to be one gated tourist package hotel after another but these diminish as you head further up the coast road to **Matemwe**, a small village 45 km from Stone Town and 15 km north of Kiwengwa. Inland from Matemwe, is some of the most fertile land on the island, a centre for rice, sugar and cassava production. Matemwe beach itself makes few concessions to tourists in that it's a centre for gathering seaweed and fishing. Depending on the position of the tide, you'll either see scores of women wading fully dressed into the sea to collect their daily crop or fleets of dhows sailing away to fish. It's one of the most interesting stretches of coast on the island and beautiful in the way that its very much a locals' place carrying on their traditional way of life. About 1 km off the coast of Matemwe lies the small island of **Mnemba**. About 500 m in diameter, the island, surrounded by a circular coral reef, is renowned for its diving and game fishing. It is privately leased and to visit it is necessary to stay in the exclusive lodge (see below).

To the northeast coast listings

For Sleeping and Eating price codes and other relevant information, see pages 12-17.

For Sleeping and Eating price codes and other relevant information, see pages 12-17.

⊖ Sleeping

North of Chwaka *p97*
Uroa

$$$ Zanzibar Safari Club, T0777-844482 (mob), sales@hotelsandlodges-tanzania.com. Recently acquired by the Hotels and Lodges Tanzania group, there are 50 rooms in bandas in the gardens here. The resort has very brightly painted decor throughout, there's a dive school, tennis courts, 3 bars, 1 of which is at the end of a wooden pier out to sea where they have a disco, 2 restaurants, internet café and tours desk.

$$ Tamarind Beach Hotel, T0777-411191 (mob), www.tamarind.nu. This lodge has a relaxed and informal atmosphere, with 18 simple bungalows near the beach with own bathrooms, nets and ceiling fans. European-run, with a pleasant restaurant that has an exensive menu and open-air bar. They can arrange diving at Mnemba Atoll, snorkelling, game fishing, bike hire for US$10, and massages. Free internet. Their new pool should be ready for summer 2009 and they offer good reductions for low season

Pongwe

$$$ Pongwe Beach Hotel, T0773-662579 (mob), www.pongwe.com. Nice stone and thatch beach bungalows with en suite bathrooms, Zanzibari beds with mosquito nets, and fans, set in lovely relaxing gardens. Attractive swimming pool area with decking overlooking the beach. They allow day visitors to use the pool, but limit this to 4 a day with a minimum spend of US$25 per person.The English consultant chef used to work at the Dorchester Hotel in London. Internet available. Can arrange all the usual tours, snorkelling and game fishing.

Kiwengwa

$$$$ Bluebay Beach Resort, T024-224 0240 /4, www.bluebayzanzibar.com. Completely refurbished in 2008, this all round quality family resort on a lovely stretch of beach has 112 rooms ranging from ultra-luxurious Sultan's Suites to pretty garden rooms with en suite bathrooms and sea views, 4-poster beds, a/c, mosquito nets, satellite TV and minibar. There are several restaurants and bars, swimming pool, fitness centre, tennis court, children's club, watersports. **One Ocean Diving** have a base here.

$$$$ Shooting Star Inn, on headland at the north end of the beach, a 15-min walk along the road or beach from the village, T0787-195029 (mob), www.shootingstarlodge.com. Still owned by the charismatic Ali who opened this lodge 13 years ago as the first in Kiwengwa, it is now surrounded by land belonging to the luxury **Zamani Zanzibar Kempinski**. Thankfully, he's declined to sell his property to his new neighbour because it's a beautiful, intimate place to stay with 16 rooms ranging from pretty garden lodge rooms to top-class luxury suites with private pools. All are furnished in Zanzibari style and the suites, spread out over 3 floors with a rooftop sunbathing area, are stunning. Open-air bar and restaurant on sand and with makuti roof is very atmospheric and serves seafood, grills and traditional Zanzibari cuisine – some of the best food to be had on the east coast. Meals are included in the room rates. Bicycles for hire and there is a lovely salt water infinity pool 10 m above the beach. Recommended.

$$$$ Zamani Zanzibar Kempinski, just off the main road from Pongwe to Kiwengwa, T024-224 0066, www.kempinski-zanzibar.com. Set in 12 ha of gardens, this is one of the newer – and more expensive – of Zanzibar's hotels, with 110 rooms and 7 private suites. The hotel has all the luxury facilities you'd expect of a Kempinski, with a 60 m infinity pool, a lap pool in the fitness suite, and private pools for each of the 7 villas. There's a private beach about 1 km away from the main hotel at the Zamani Beach Club (beyond the **Shooting Star Inn**), and there are several bars, including a very attractive bar on a jetty over the ocean, and restaurants serving top of the range international cuisine. Double rooms from US$330, suites from US$670-$6700. See website for special offers.

Pwani Mchangani

$$$$ Mapenzi Beach Resort, 2 km south of Pwani Mchangani Village, roughly half way between Matemwe and Kiwengwa, T0774-414268 (mob), www.planhotel.ch. All-inclusive resort with watersports centre, good food, 87 a/c rooms, Swahili decor, set in 4 ha of gardens, swimming pool, shops, internet café and tennis courts. Rates include all meals and alcoholic drinks and activities such as windsurfing and canoeing, but diving and fishing are extra. Popular with Italians and Swiss. Most people book through tour operators but they will take 'walk-in' guests on a fully inclusive basis only.

$$$ Mchanga Beach Lodge, just outside the village, signposted on the right heading towards Matemwe, T0773-569821 (mob), www.mchangabeachlodge.com. A small, intimate lodge, with 6 sea view lodge rooms and 2 garden suites, all set in pretty gardens opening on to the beach. A quiet, low-key place with a pool right by the beach and nearby an open-air restaurant specializing in Swahili cuisine and seafood. Internet available, tours and diving can be arranged.

Mnemba Island

$$$$ Mnemba Island Lodge, central reservations, South Africa, T+27-11-809 4300, www.andbeyond.com. Mnemba Island lies 4.5 km or 15 mins by boat from northeast Zanzibar. This beautiful little private island has a reputation as one of the world's finest beach retreats and is impossibly romantic. Very stylish, very discreet and very expensive. The coral reef that circles the island is the finest in Zanzibar. 10 self-contained cottages, full board accommodation, includes most watersports and big game fishing. The US magazine, *Travel & Leisure* said of it, "It's the closest two people can get to being shipwrecked, with no need for rescue." If you can afford it, enjoy. Rates are over US$1200 per person in high season, fully inclusive of meals with house wines, and all watersports including 2 dives a day providing you have a PADI certificate.

Matemwe

$$$$ Azanzi Beach Village, turn right along main road in village, signposted on the right, just north of Matemwe Beach Village, T0772-284346 (mob), www.azanzibeachhotel.com. Opened in Dec 2008, this classy boutique hotel has 35 well-appointed rooms furnished in a contemporary style with lovely Zanzibari touches, including locally carved wood furniture and doors. The bathrooms have huge showers (some have outdoor showers too) and free-standing baths. Rooms are accessed by wooden walkways through lush gardens and the Mnemba View bar and Bridge restaurant on the 1st floor of the main building have great views. There's also a bar by the swimming pool just back from the beach, a games room, TV lounge, internet access and spa. Check out their glass-bottomed kayaks for a different perspective on exploring the sea and coral. Room rates flexible depending on season.

$$$$ Fairmont Zanzibar, about 1 km to the south of the village, T024-224 0391, www.fair

mont.com/zanzibar. A very stylish, new hotel with 99 rooms and 10 suites, this is one of the more attractive of the larger hotels in the region. The rooms are spread out in beautiful gardens, some with direct access to the beach, with colourful decor, a/c, satellite TV, nets and private verandas. There are 2 beachside pools here, 2 restaurants (the intimate Zama Grill restaurant up on the first floor has great views over the ocean), a spa and a fabulous cocktail bar just above the beach. It also has its own dive centre (complete with decompression chamber), and offers a whole range of water sports from kitesurfing to deep-sea fishing. Check website for early booking discounts.

$$$$ Matemwe Bungalows/Matemwe Retreat, at the far north of the beach, www.asilialodges.com. A luxury lodge with adjacent private villas, impeccable service and beautiful accommodation, opposite Mnemba Atoll. The lodge has 12 bungalows all with private verandas, and hammocks that overlook the sea (as does the infinity pool). The 3 private villas at Matemwe Retreat have their own pools on their roof terraces and guests here can choose whether to have dinner in their private gardens or go to the restaurant at Matemwe Bungalows, which specializes in seafood. Privacy comes at a price – US$525 per person for the villas, while the bungalows are US$310 per person.

$$$ Matemwe Baharini Villas, north of the village, T0777-417768 (mob), www.matemwevillas.com. 15 stone bungalows with makuti roofs. Don't be too put off by the untidy screens on the outside of the windows – inside the rooms are fine, with a/c, fans, mosquito nets and TV. There's a decentsized swimming pool overlooking the beach and a cavernous open-air restaurant.

$$$ Matemwe Beach Village, to the north of the village, signposted as you enter, on the right heading north, T024-223 8374, www. matemwebeach.com. One of the nicest

places to stay in Matemwe, with friendly staff, 16 pretty rooms, 5 suites and great food. Its strongest point is its chilled atmosphere. The swimming pool cascades into another pool below, conveniently close to the bar and BBQ area where dinner is served twice a week. The main restaurant is near the beach, as are some of the rooms, with others located further back in the gardens. There are some lovely touches here, like the sunrise tea and coffee on the beach if you make the effort to get up early, the Dhow Lounge above the pool furnished with old dhows, the honeymoon suite with its own private chef and beach area, and the free dhow trip that takes residents up to the reef at full tide. **One Ocean Diving** operate from here and offer PADI courses and diving trips to Mnemba Atoll, see www.zanzibaroneocean.com. Good value. Recommended.

$$$ Zanzibar Retreat, signposted to the right as you enter Matemwe, T0776-108379 (mob) www.zanzibarretreat.com. With a very hospitable Finnish manager, this small but beautifully appointed hotel has just 7 rooms around the edge of the main house and feels like a home-from-home. There's a good sized pool near the beach and a relaxing bar, and the place is very much a 'foodie' delight. The rooms are elegant with sleek hardwood furniture and floorings. Staff can arrange all the usual tours but the hotel also has an interesting Community Programme of village walkabouts, coral reef and seaweed safaris, and visits to a local women's group working on alternative energy projects – with money from the proceeds supporting the village.

$$ Nyota Beach Bungalows, on the beach to the south of Matemwe Village, T0777-439059 (mob), www.nyotabeachbungalows.com. A relaxing place with 10 rooms in 4 bungalows mostly in gardens set back from the beach, although one overlooks the sea. All rooms have fans, mosquito nets and bathrooms, and are simply furnished and clean. There's a nice bar under a makuti roof and a restaurant that serves reasonable food. Friendly staff.

$ Keys Bungalows, on beach further north from **Mohammed's Bungalows**, T0777-411797 (mob), allykeys786@yahoo.com. A low-budget option with plenty of character, there are 6 rustic bungalows here, simply but nicely furnished with sturdy padlocks on cupboards made from old dhows for security. US$50 for a double with breakfast. There's a cool seating area outside with hammocks and loungers, and the bar right on the beach plays reggae music, serves fresh fish, and uses more old dhows for furniture. Very chilled atmosphere.

$ Mohammed's Bungalows, just north of **Azanzi Beach Village**, on the beach, T0777-431881 (mob). A decent low-budget option with just 4 bungalows right on the beach. Each has its own bathroom and is clean but basic with mosquito nets and fans for US$20 per person including breakfast. There's also a small restaurant here that serves straightforward meals like chicken and fresh fish.

⊛ Festivals and events

To the northeast coast *p96*
See page 81 for information on festivals which are held throughout the archipelago.

Southeast Zanzibar

To get to the southeast of the island leave Stone Town's Creek Road at the junction that leads out through the Michenzani housing estate. Eventually the houses begin to peter out and are replaced by small fields of cassava, maize, banana and papaya. The road continues via Tunguu and Bungi to the Jozani Forest near Pete, before joining the coastal road linking the resorts of Jambiani, Paje and Bwejuu, about 50 km from Stone Town. There is a magnificent beach here that runs for nearly 20 km from Bwejuu to Jambiani, with white sand backed for its whole length by palm trees, laced with incredibly picturesque lagoons. You will see the fishermen go out in their dhows, while the women sit in the shade and plait coconut fibre, which they then make into everything from fishing nets to beds.

Ins and outs

Getting there There's a good tarmac road that leads from Stone Town to Paje. The trip there by minibus takes just over an hour and costs around US$10. Bus No 9 from the Creek Road in Stone Town serves Paje and continues to Jambiani and Bwejuu. Bus No 10 from Creek Road goes to Kizimkazi via Jambiani and Makunduchi.

Jozani Forest

ⓘ *Most people visit the reserve as part of a tour, usually combined with a dolphin tour, but you can get here independently by* dala-dala *and either bus No 9 or 10 from Creek Road in Stone Town. Going there by taxi will cost around US$40 (for 4 people in 1 car), which is competitive with the price of an organized tour.*

Most of Zanzibar's indigenous forests have been lost to agriculture or construction, but the Jozani Forest in the centre of Zanzibar has been declared a protected reserve. It covers 44 sq km, roughly 3% of the whole island. It is 24 km southeast of Stone Town, an easy stop-off en route to the southeast coast beaches. It is home to roughly one third of the remaining endemic Zanzibar red colobus monkeys, one of Africa's rarest primates. Only 1500 are believed to have survived. In Zanzibar the Kiswahili name for the red colobus monkey is *Kima Punju* – 'Poison Monkey'. It has associations with the kind of poisons used by evil doers. Local people believe that when the monkeys have fed in an area, the trees and crops die, and dogs will lose their hair if they eat the colobus. Although legally protected the colobus remain highly endangered. Their choice of food brings them into conflict with the farmers, and their habitat is being destroyed due to demands for farmland, fuel, wood and charcoal. The monkeys appear oblivious to tourists, swinging above the trees in troups of about 40, babies to adults. They are endearing, naughty and totally absorbing. There is a **visitor centre** on the main road to the south where you pay US$10 per person for a guide for the 45 minute nature trail through the forest. The reserve is completely managed by the local people who operate tree nurseries and act as rangers and guides. Stout shoes are recommended as there are some venomous snakes. Lizards, civets, mongooses and Ader's duiker are plentiful and easy to see, and there are also Sykes' monkey, bush babies, hyraxes, and over 50 species of butterfly and 40 species of birds. Unless you state otherwise you are unlikely to be taken into the reserve at all as the best place to get close to the monkeys is an area adjacent to farmland to the south of the road.

On the way to Jozani Forest from Stone Town, you can visit the **Zanzibar Butterfly Centre** ⓘ *T0773-999897 (mob), www.zanzibarbutterflies.com, daily 0900-1700, entry US$5, the butterflies are most active between 1030-1530*. This is a great new centre where the funds generated help local communities and conservation. They have a colourful collection of Tanzanian butterflies, often in their hundreds, farmed sustainably in the nearby villages and provide tours lasting around half an hour to explain the project and the butterfly's life cycle.

About 1 km south of the Jozani Forest Visitor Centre there is the **Pete-Jozani Mangrove Boardwalk**. From the visitor centre the walk takes you through coral forest to an old tamarind tree, which marks the beginning of the boardwalk. The transition from coral forest to mangroves is abrupt. The boardwalk, which is horseshoe shaped, takes you through the mangrove swamp. Mangroves anchor the shifting mud and sands of the shore and help prevent coastal erosion. There are 18,000 ha of mangrove forests along the muddy coasts and inlets of Zanzibar. When the tide is out the stilt-like roots of the trees are visible. Crabs and fish are plentiful and easily seen from the boardwalk. The construction costs of the boardwalk were paid for by the government of The Netherlands, with local communities providing labour. Part of the profits made from tourists is returned directly to the local villagers.

ZALA Park

The road continues south to the village of Kitogani, and just south is **ZALA Park** ① *US$5*, which is primarily a small educational facility set up in conjunction with the University of Dar es Salaam for Zanzibari children to help them learn about and conserve the island's fauna. ZALA stands for Zanzibar Land Animals. Entry is free to local children if they are unable to pay, subsidized by the tourists' donations. The aim is to make it a self-funding enterprise in time. There is a small classroom where the children are taught. The adjacent **zoo** has a number of reptiles, including lizards, chameleons and indolent rock pythons weighing up to 40 kg, Eastern tree hyrax, as well as Suni antelopes, an endemic Zanzabari subspecies. Donations to support this worthwhile enterprise are appreciated.

Paje

Paje is the first village on the coast you are likely to get to as it lies on the junction with the direct road from Stone Town. It has its share of guesthouses and there is an old mausoleum, a long, low rectangular building with castellations and old plates and dishes set into the walls. This design, along with other reliefs and designs used in the villages are of typical Shirazi origin and indicate that this area was settled very early in Zanzibar's history. There's a convenient little supermarket in Paje on the main road as you enter the village which has a post office, a small café, does takeaway cooked food and can even provide car and bike hire.

Bwejuu

Bwejuu is best known for its proximity to 'the lagoon' and the Chwaka Bay mangrove swamps. The mangrove swamp at Chwaka Bay can be reached by a small road leading inland from the back of Bwejuu Village. It is possible to find a guide locally, who can navigate the way through the maze of channels and rivers in the swamps. Here you can stroll through the shallow rivers looking at this uniquely adapted plant and its ecosystem, there is also a good chance of seeing a wide variety of crabs that live in the mud-banks amongst the tangle of roots. The best snorkelling in the area is to be found at 'the lagoon', about 3 km to the north of Bwejuu, just past the pier at Dongwe. Bicycles and snorkels can usually be hired from any of the children on the beach.

Michamvi

Michamvi is a small village right at the tip of the eastern peninsula, another 5 km north of Dongwe and about 68 km from Stone Town. A handful of mid-range hotels and lodges have opened here recently and the area still has an 'off the beaten track' feel to it. A couple of new developments are being built on the western side of the peninsula, one of which is rumoured to be a five-star resort owned by the President's daughter. Local transport only goes as far as Bwejuu, so you'd need to arrange a taxi or car through your hotel.

Jambiani

The name Jambiani comes from an Arabic word for dagger, and legend has it that early settlers found a dagger here in the sand – evidence of previous visitors. These days the village spreads for several kilometres along the coast road and there are a number of resorts (see Sleeping below).

Kizimkazi

This small fishing village was once the site of a town built by King Kizi and his mason Kazi from whom the name Kizimkazi originates. Most people visit here as part of a tour to swim with the dolphins and there is a growing industry springing up around the large resident pods of humpbacked and bottlenose dolphins.

WMarine biologists assess these dolphins as being very stressed by the uncontrolled jostling and chasing of boat operators. They advise that if you snorkel with these dolphins you exercise respect, restraint and common sense. Splashy water entries and boat drivers in hot pursuit will only drive them away.

The beach is attractive and there is a restaurant where those on dolphin tours from Stone Town are often taken to have a meal. A few hotels have opened here in recent years as people realize this is a pretty location in its own right, aside from being the centre of the dolphin-swimming industry on the island. The village is split into two parts, Kizimkazi Dimbani in the north and Kizimkazi Mkunguni in the south. Other than when the dolphin-trippers come in the mornings, it's a fairly quiet area, so if you're after a lively night scene, this wouldn't be your best option, apart from between Boxing Day and New Year's Day when the new Kizimkazi Cultural Music Festival takes place (see **Promised Land**, page 110, and Festivals and events, page 110). The **Shirazi Dimbani Mosque ruins** are near Kizimkazi and contain the oldest inscription found in East Africa – from AD 1107. The mosque has been given a tin roof and is still used. However, its significance should not be under-estimated for it may well mark the beginnings of the Muslim religion in East Africa. It was built by Sheikh Abu bin Mussa Lon Mohammed and archaeologists believe that it stands on the site of an even older mosque.

Southeast Zanzibar listings

For Sleeping and Eating price codes and other relevant information, see pages 12-17.

● Sleeping

Paje *p104*

$$$ Arabian Nights, on the beach near **Paje by Night**, T024-224 0190, www.zanzibararabiannights.com. Rooms are in stone cottages either facing the beach or around the garden or pool and are well-equipped with spacious bathrooms, private terraces, TVs, mosquito nets, fans and a/c. There's also a nearby block with rooms for gap year groups which are let out to individual

travellers when there are vacancies. These are really good value at US$40-65 for a double and this block has its own pool. The owner, Mohammed, also owns the new **Buccaneer Diving Centre** which is about to open here, just down the beach from the hotel. It promises to be the biggest diving centre in Tanzania with 2 restaurants and a training pool and will offer a whole range of PADI courses and water sports including kitesurfing.

$$$ Hakuna Majiwe, on the borders of Paje and Jambiani, signposted off the main road, T0777-515371 (mob), www.hakunamajiwe. net. A boutique lodge set on the beach with

20 individual and very attractively decorated rooms in stone bandas, surrounded by palms and shrubs and sand. The swimming pool's set back from the beach and there's a huge, open dining area with big sofas at the bar. Wi-Fi available. Snorkelling and diving centre.

$$$ Kinazi Upepo and **Cristal Resort**, at the end of the group of lodges on the beach, T0777-875515 (mob), www.cristalresort.net. These 2 properties more or less merge into 1 and share facilities in a pretty location surrounded by palm trees and pines. They have 25 single and 40 double rooms either in de luxe bungalows or in attractively rustic 'eco' bungalows which are cheaper but nicer, all with fans, mosquito nets and bathrooms. **Cristal** has a swimming pool near the beach and there's a very chilled bar at **Kinezi**.

$$$ Paje by Night, on the beach in the village centre, T0777-460710 (mob), www.pajebynight.net. Very rustic verging on ethnic, run by an Italian. Self-contained thatched bungalows with ceiling fans and mosquito nets, including a useful family bungalow with 2 double en suite rooms. Bar and restaurant with local and international food including good pizzas. An unashamed party place, bar stays open all night, hence the name.

$$ Paradise Beach Bungalows, 1 km north of the village, T024-223 1387, www.geocities.jp/paradisebeachbungalows. Run by a nice (but scatty) Japanese lady, Saori. There are 10 en suite double rooms and 3 bandas sharing bathrooms a small restaurant and bar serving expensive Japanese meals that must be ordered in advance. Rates are between US$28-50 per person including breakfast.

Bwejuu *p104*

$$$$ Breezes Beach Club, 3.5 km north of the village, T024-224 0102 www.breezes-zanzibar.com. This well-appointed resort is an established favourite on Zanzibar. All 70 rooms have a/c, fans and en suite bath-rooms. There are standard, de luxe and superior de luxe rooms, the latter have sea views, with either balconies or terraces. Shopping arcade, beauty spa, conference facilities, restaurants, bars, large swimming pool, fitness centre, watersports centre, tennis courts and disco. The **Rising Sun Dive Centre** is based here. Rates vary depending on the season.

$$$$ Karafuu Hotel Beach Resort, 3 km north of the village before Michamvi, in Karafuu Village, T0777-413647-8 (mob), www.karafuuzanzibar.com. The name means 'cloves' in Swahili. Winner of 4 awards, including 'The Best Resort in Tanzania 2008', this is a large but quiet and professionally run resort, with almost 100 a/c rooms with thatched roofs in spacious gardens. 3 restaurants, numerous bars, watersports, excellent food, swimming pool, tennis courts, nightclub and diving.The beach is good although watch out for the very sharp coral close offshore.

$$$$ The Palms, a few kilometres north of Bwejuu towards Pingwe, reservations, Nairobi, T+254-20-272 9333, www.palms-zanzibar.com. Stunning resort, super-luxurious with attentive service. At US$650 per person you'd expect nothing less, but rates are inclusive of meals, soft drinks, house wine, and return airport transfers. For your money you get a villa with satellite TV, DVD player, private terrace with plunge pool, living room and bar. Facilities in sumptuous surroundings include tiered swimming pool, beauty spa, fitness centre, tennis court, elegant dining room, bars and lounge areas. The beach here is magnificent and there's a watersports centre and dive school.

$$$ Echo Beach, signposted off the main road to Paje, just south of Breezes T0773-593260 (mob), www.echobeachhotel.com. Owned by a British couple, one a French-trained chef and the other an interior designer, this place is as you might expect very stylish with an excellent restaurant menu. All 12 rooms in local stone and makuti bungalows, are individually designed with African antiques, silk fabrics and locally crafted wooden furniture, with spacious verandas. The swimming pool and jacuzzi are near the beach and the lodge has its own dive centre.

$$$ Sunrise Guest House, 2 km north of the village, T0777-415240 (mob), www.sunrise- zanzibar.com. All bungalow rooms are self-contained with fans and mosquito nets, and face towards the sea. Very good food, especially the chocolate mousse, courtesy of the Belgian chef/owner. Bikes can be hired and there's a swimming pool.

$$ Evergreen Bungalows, 3 km north of Bwejuu Village, T024-224 0273, www.ever green-bungalows.com. 9 bungalows in a palm grove directly on the beach with 14 rooms, each with a different touch and very nicely decorated using local materials, with mosquito nets, solar power supply and balcony with chairs and a table. Some rooms are self-contained while others, including some dorm rooms, have shared bathrooms. Bar and restaurant offers a meat, fish and vegetarian dish each night for dinner. **Africa Blue Divers** offer single dives from US$50 and a PADI Open Water Course for US$400.

$$ Mustapha's Place (although the sign outside says **Mustapha's Nest**), in the village, the No 9 bus will drop you outside, T024-224 0069, www.mustaphasplace.com. A chilled out, low budget hotel run by Mustapha, a friendly Rastafarian. Lovely gardens with hammocks, reggae music, bar where you can play drums, good seafood. The rooms are fun and bright, with paintings on the walls and 1 called Treetops is on huge stilts. Prices range from US$35 for a double room with shared bathroom, to US$55 for a double room with bathroom, although some rooms can sleep up to 8 people with floor space in the loft and can then work out a lot cheaper. Very relaxing, it's across the road from the beach and a pretty pathway leads you to it.

$ Robinson's Place, 2 km north of Bwejuu, take the road signposted to Evergreen, go past **Evergreen** and Robinson's is on the right when you reach some palm raffia fencing and gates on both sides, T0777-413479 (mob), www.robinsonsplace.net. In a similar vein to **Mustapha's**, but smaller with a maximum of 10 guests, and run by the charming Rastafarian Eddy and his wife Ann. It's essential to book here because it fills up very quickly. All rooms have nets and some have bathrooms. There's no electricity here, just solar power and a generator, and they serve local Zanzibari food (with floor seating) for a very reasonable US$6.

Michamvi p104

$$$ Kichanga Lodge, signposted off main road to Michamvi, then 1 km along dirt road, T0773-175124 (mob), www.kichanga.com. British owned and Italian managed, this sleepy place is in a secluded beach location with 23 pretty bungalows spread out in gardens. The Ocean Villas have a mezzanine floor with extra beds which overlook the ground floor bedroom and share their bathroom, so if you want privacy, that may not be the best set-up. But they're nice rooms, with fans, mosquito nets and private terraces. The bar and dining area is in a breezy makuti-roofed building with a mezzanine lounge that has great views over the ocean. For a more unusual souvenir, their gift shop makes up dresses to order in contemporary styles out of traditional *kangas* in 24 hrs. Massage centre, mountain bikes and canoes for hire. They also have their own dhow for snorkelling excursions and can arrange all the usual tours.

$$$ Michamvi Water Sports Resort, Michamvi Village, there's a faded sign on the right which leads along a dirt road, then turn left at a better signpost, T0777-878136 (mob), www.michamvi.com. This is not the easiest place to find but the manager has promised better signage. As the name suggests, the activities at this new hotel are very much water based – they offer waterskiing, parasailing, windsurfing, kitesurfing, paddle skis, kayaking, wakeboarding, etc, and arrange diving and deep-sea fishing through a Paje outfit. Their 20 attractive rooms are in 4 blocks facing the sea and the swimming pool, all with a balcony or terrace, a/c, fans and mosquito nets, and old dhows are used as furniture. The bar and restaurant serves international cuisine.

$$$ Ras Michamvi Beach Resort, signposted with **Kichanga Lodge** off the main road to Michamvi, then 1 km down a dirt road and follow the signs. T024-223 1081, www.rasmichamvi.com. This is a discreet and very pretty new lodge right at the tip of the peninsula. The 15 en suite rooms are in 4 stone bungalows with cool tiled flooring, a/c, fans, mosquito nets and big Zanzibari beds. There are 3 small beaches here, 1 of which – Coconut Beach – has resident red colobus monkeys and fossils have been found amid the coral. It's also a great spot for sundowners. Nice swimming pool above the beach and an outdoor gym. The restaurant is open to non-residents and in the season they have Swahili entertainment – Bi Kidude, the queen of Taarab music has played here. Good value at US$140 for a double half board.

Jambiani p105

$$$ Kikadini Villas, next door to **Hotel Casa del Mar** on the beach, T0777-707888 (mob), www.kikadinivillas.com. 5 villas beautifully decorated in understated Zanzibari style right on the beach that can be booked for exclusive use or as individual rooms. They sleep from 2-6 people if booked exclusively, and Villa Maroc is particularly suitable for loved-up couples, having a private roof terrace and bath to soak in under the stars. If booked exclusively, you get full butler service and meals are served in your villa or there's a candlelit restaurant for dinner.

$$$ Sau Inn, T024-224 0169, www.sauinn zanzibar.com. A pleasant, friendly hotel with 39 en suite rooms set in thatched cottages with fans and mosquito nets. The upstairs bar has a nice terrace overlooking the beach and the restaurant serves good seafood and generous portions, with buffets on Fri evenings. There's a swimming pool just back from the beach and snorkelling and diving are available from the hotel's own dive centre. B&B, half- or full-board rates. Good value.

$$ Blue Oyster Hotel, T024-224 0163, www.zanzibar.de. Very congenial, Tanzanian owned, hotel. The 13 rooms have beautiful carved beds, mosquito nets, and are arranged around a serene ornamental pool and garden. Good food in the rooftop restaurant. Bike rental, watersports, their own dhow for fishing and snorkelling trips. An en suite double is US$80 and doubles without bathrooms are US$42, including breakfast.

$$ Coco Beach, on the beach in Jambiani Village, T0773-492670 (mob), cocobeach@ zitec.org. Self-contained rooms with hot water, fan and mosquito nets. Good restaurant serving reasonably priced seafood, and bar. US$50 for a double including breakfast. Can arrange tours and activities.

$$ Coral Rocks, just south of Jambiani Village on a coral rock above the sea, T024-224 0154, www.coralrockhotel zanzibar.com. Rooms here are slightly tired but have nice Zanzibari beds, nets, a/c, fans and bathrooms. There'sa pleasant swimming pool on the edge ofthe beach and a popular bar nearby.

$$ Hotel Casa del Mar, next to the internet café in Jambiani Village, on the beach, T024-224 0400, www.casa-delmar-zanzibar. com. This hotel has an excellent restaurant and bar and although the service is sometimes slow, it's worth the wait for the generous portions and the fresh non-alcoholic cocktails (highly recommended). 12 rustic rooms in

2 buildings on 2 floors, all en suite with sea views. US$80 for a double on the ground floor and US$100 on the 1st floor where rooms are bigger with a sleeping gallery on the mezzanine. Rates include breakfast.

$$ Visitor's Inn, T024-224 0150, www.visitorsinn-zanzibar.com. 39 basic but good value rooms either in the guesthouse or bungalows set in flowering gardens, each has a fridge, hot water, a fan, mosquito net and a porch. TV room, restaurant and bar with fish, noodle and vegetarian dishes, internet.

$ Red Monkey Lodge, Jambiani Village, on the beach, T024-224 0207, www.zanzibar-jambiani.com. This is a fun place, rooms are in white-washed stone cottages with makuti roofs and have their own bathrooms, fans and mosquito nets. They're a bit scruffy but in a lovely location on a gentle slope above the beach and cost US$50 for a double, including breakfast and light snacks which are served from lunchtime until 1700. Evening meals are charged separately. There's a happy, lively atmosphere here and the place is named after a red monkey that lives in the gardens.

Kizimkazi p105

$$$$ Unguja Resort, in Kizimkazi Mikunga, T0774-855868 (mob), www.unguja resort.com. A very atmospheric, discreet resort set in tropical gardens with huge baobab trees and palms, it's an expensive but beautiful place. Accommodation is in 10 stunningly designed cottages with makuti roofs and curved walls, semi-outdoor living rooms and bathing areas, and a spacious bedroom indoors, with another bed on the mezzanine level. Most cottages have sea views with private terraces but the 3 that don't have their own jacuzzis as compensation. If you can tear yourself away from your cottage, there's a large swimming pool and a coral beach, and the owner's son acts as guide on coral reef walks. **One Ocean** looks after all their diving requirements.

$$$ Dolphin Beach Hotel, to the south of Kizimkazi Dimbani, T024-224 0348, www.dolphinbeach-resort.com. There are 33 en suite rooms here in rondavaals with makuti roofs, most with a sea view and all with a small garden and beachy terrace outside. Simply furnished with Zanzibari beds, fans and mosquito nets. Unusually there is a huge natural cave here where wooden decking and electricity have been installed, making an atmospheric venue for Swahili dance and food evenings or for private parties. There are 2 swimming pools, (1 shallow for families) and they can arrange all the usual trips and deep-sea fishing.

$$$ Karamba, Kizimkazi Dimbani beach, at the northern end, T0773-166406 (mob), www.karambaresort.com. This lovely, laid-back lodge has its own yoga teacher and offers various yoga classes, Ayurvedic massage and even Vedic options on its extensive restaurant menu (over 100 dishes), which also includes sushi and sashimi, Indian, Italian and tapas. The 14 en suite rooms are on a small cliff above the sea, all have fans and mosquito nets and are pleasantly decorated. There's a natural swimming pool here in the sea at high tide, with steps down the cliff straight into the water, although they are also planning a 'normal' pool for Aug 2009. They support the local school and guests are able to visit and work there for a day if they wish.

$$$ Swahili Beach Resort, Kizimkazi Mkunguni, T024-224 04913, www.swahili beachresort.com. A sister hotel to **Arabian Nights** in Paje (see page 105) and almost identical in appearance and facilities, they have 19 rooms in stone bungalows, as well as guesthouse rooms for gap year groups, which again represent good value for independent travellers if they're available. Swimming pool, PADI diving centre, internet and the usual tours and excursions. There are more charismatic places to stay perhaps, but good value.

$$ Kizimkazi Coral Reef Bungalows, in Kizimkazi Mkunguni, near **Swahili Beach Resort**, T0777-479615 (mob), www.coral reefzanzibar.com. 6 simple but clean rooms in pretty palm gardens with own bathrooms, Zanzibari beds and mosquito nets. The restaurant is very reasonably priced and overlooks the bay. Chilled atmosphere and good value.

$ Promised Land, about 20 mins walk (1 km) from Kizimkazi Mkunguni Village, past Swahili Beach turn left after 0.5 km, then right after another 0.5 km, signposted, T0783-576036 (mob), shaaban1976@ hotmail.com.This is a very chilled place, owned and run by a Rastafarian called Shaaban. Offers 4 double rooms with own bathrooms, fans and mosquito nets in the main house for US$40, and a dorm-style mezzanine floor above the dining/living room, accessed by steep wooden steps, which has 5 single beds for (a rather pricey) US$20 a person. There's also a huge field where 6 tents have been set up under raffia shelters (US$15 per person) and plenty of space for people to bring their own tents. All rates include breakfast and there's a beach bar, restaurant and hammocks for hanging out. If you're into music festivals, then you should come between Boxing Day and New Year's Day when Shaaban hosts the **Kizimkazi Cultural Music Festival**, see below.

❂ Festivals and events

Southeast Zanzibar *p102*
See also page 81for more information on festivals held throughout the archipelago.

Jul Mwaka Kogwa, held in the 3rd week of Jul. The traditional Shirazi New Year on Zanzibar and celebrated with traditional Swahili food, taraab music, drumming and dancing on the beach all night. Although the festival is celebrated around the island, the village of Makunduchi is the heart of the celebration. The men of the village have a play fight and beat each other with banana fronds to vent their aggressions from the past year. Then, the *mganga*, or traditional healer, sets fire to a ritual hut and reads which way the smoke is burning to determine the village's prosperity in the coming year.

Dec Kizimkazi Cultural Music Festival, starts on Boxing Day and concludes in a great finale on New Year's Eve/Day. Attracts musicians, taarab bands, drummers, dancers and acrobats from mainland Tanzania and Kenya as well as local Zanzibaris. It's held at the Promised Land (see Sleeping, above). The first festival in 2008 was a success, despite a few teething problems like the generator blowing, and they're now planning to make this an annual event. Reports welcome.

▲ Activities and tours

Kizimkazi *p105*
Diving
One Ocean, various bases all over the island, T024-223 8374, www.zanzibaroneocean.com.

Pemba Island

Unlike Unguja, which is flat and sandy, Pemba's terrain is hilly, fertile and heavily vegetated. The early Arab sailors called it 'Al Huthera', meaning 'The Green Island'. Today more cloves are grown on Pemba than on Zanzibar Island. Pemba has a wealth of natural resources ranging from beaches to mangrove ecosystems to natural forests. The coral reefs surrounding the island protect a multitude of marine species and offer some of the best scuba-diving in the world. Zanzibar Island is connected to the African continent by a shallow submerged shelf. Pemba, however, is separated from the mainland by depths of over 1000 m. During September and March the visibility around Pemba has been known to extend to a depth of 50 m and there are great game fish such as sharks, tuna, marlin and barracuda. While much of the coast is lined with mangroves, there are a few good stretches of shoreline and attractive offshore islands with pure, clean beaches and interesting birdlife. There are also some important ruins and charming Swahili villages. The tourism industry here is still in its infancy and the infrastructure is still quite basic, but is slowly beginning to develop, with new lodges opening up and a few more foreigners visiting than before, although nothing on the scale of visitors to Zanzibar.

Ins and outs

Getting there
Pemba Airport is 7 km to the southeast of Chake Chake. The island can be reached by air either from Zanzibar Island or from Dar es Salaam, though most flights from Dar go via Zanzibar. Coastal Air also fly direct between Tanga and Pemba. The airport tax for flights out of Pemba is US$2.50 but this is payable in Tanzanian Shillings and may be included in your ticket price. Public transport from the airport only operates when there is a flight due.

Ferries to Pemba can be unreliable, often cancelled at the last minute, uncomfortable and often with very bumpy crossings. Nearly all ferries coming into Pemba arrive at the town of Mkoani, on the southwestern end of Pemba Island. Very few ships or dhows actually use Chake Chake anymore, as the old harbour is silted up and only canoes can actually gain entrance. The journey between Zanzibar and Pemba can take between three and six hours depending on the company and boats used, and prices are about US$40 excluding Zanzibar's port tax of US$5. Dar es Salaam to Pemba via Zanzibar US$65.
➤➤ For further details, see Transport, page 119.

Getting around
The island of Pemba is about 70 km long and 22 km wide. There is one bumpy main road in Pemba running from Msuka in the north to Mkoani in the south, which is served by public transport. There are buses or *dala-dala* along the main roads but these tend to operate in the mornings and early afternoons only and there are very few vehicles after 1500. *Dala-dala* No 606 runs between Chake Chake and Wete and the No 603 between Chake Chake and Mkoani. Each journey takes about one hour and costs US$0.50. Other less frequently run routes include the No 24 between Wete and Konde (for the Ngezi Forest). Besides this, it is very difficult to get around on public transport and budget travellers will need to walk to get to the more out of the way places. It is possible to hire cars at around US$80 for a day, motorcycles for around US$30 and bicycles for around US$10 – ask at the hotels and remember that negotiation is necessary, as ever. The motorcycle is the most comfortable form of transport on the island, more so than cars, as potholes are more readily avoided, and it's a little too hilly in most places for cycling.

Background

There is nothing on Pemba that holds as much historical or cultural significance as Stone Town on Zanzibar Island, but it is the site of many historical ruins that bear testament to its role in the spice trade and early commerce with the other Indian Ocean dynasties. The major income for islanders is from cloves and the island actually produces about 75-80% of the archipelago's total crop. It is the mainstay of the island's economy. Also, unlike Zanzibar, production is largely by individual small-scale farmers who own anything from 10 to 50 trees each. Most of the trees have been in the family for generations and clove production is very much a family affair, especially during the harvest when everyone joins in the picking. Harvest occurs about every five months and everything is worked around it – even the schools close. The cloves are then laid out in the sun to dry and their distinctive fragrance fills the air.

The island is overwhelmingly Muslim, with more than 95% of the population following Islam. But the island is tolerant of other cultures, and alcohol is available at hotels, some guesthouses and in the police messes (where visitors are welcome). Local inhabitants do, however, like to observe modest dress and behaviour.

Diving

Known as the Emerald Isle for its lush vegetation and idyllic setting, Pemba is most definitely the jewel in East Africa's dive-site portfolio. On the more chartered west coast the deep waters of the Pemba Channel have conspired to create dramatic walls and drop-offs, where glimpses of sharks and encounters with eagle rays, manta rays, Napoleon wrasse, great barracuda, tuna and kingfish are the norm. Visibility can range from 6 m in a plankton bloom to 60 m, though 20 m is classed as a bad day and 40 m is average. Some of the coral has been affected by El Niño, but Pemba remains a world-class diving destination.

It would be impossible to single out the best dive sites; they are all breathtaking. On Mesali Island and the surrounding reefs, the West Coast is a protected marine park and entrance of US$5 must be paid to dive or snorkel there. ▸▸ *For more information on dive operators, see page 119.*

Around the island

Pemba Channel Marine Conservation Area

Since 2006, the whole of the west coast of Pemba, from the island's northernmost tip at Ras Kigomasha to the southern tip in Panza Island, has been protected as part of a new marine conservation area known as PECCA. In all, it covers some 1000 sq km. The ultimate aim for PECCA is to have the area declared a UNESCO World Heritage Site to further protect both its marine habitats and its rich cultural heritage. All visitors to the area pay a US$5 fee, regardless of whether they dive or not.

Mkoani

Mkoani is Pemba's third largest town and the port of entry for ferries from Zanzibar and Dar es Salaam. The town is set on a hill overlooking a wide bay and comprises a mix of palm-thatch huts and rundown multi-storey apartment buildings. The landing stage is a modern jetty which projects out from the shallow beach on either side, where fishermen load their daily catch into ox-carts for the short trip to market. The main road runs directly from the port up the hill and most of this distance is rather surprisingly covered by a dual carriageway, complete with tall street lights on the central reservation. This, along with the ugly apartment blocks around town is evidence of the East German influence in Tanzania during the 1970s, which is also present at Chake Chake and Wete, and in the concrete estates on the edge of Stone Town on Zanzibar Island. Following the winding road up the hill from the port, the old colonial District Commissioners Office is on the right, where there is a bandstand in front of the compound. On the left is Ibazi Mosque, with a fine carved door. South of the dock there are steep steps down to the market by the shore.

Chake Chake

This is Pemba's main town, about halfway up the west coast of the island. The town sits on a hill overlooking a creek and is fairly small. The oldest surviving building in the town is the **Nanzim Fort,** which is thought to date back at least to the 18th century and possibly as far back as the Portuguese occupation (1499-1698). Records dating back to the early

Dive Pemba

Pemba has some of the most spectacular diving in the world. The Pemba channel separates Shimoni in Kenya from Pemba Island. The channel runs deep until it approaches the Pemba coastline and then begins a dramatic rise creating a sheer wall off the coast. Diving is characterized by crystal clear, blue water drop-offs along with pristine shallow reefs. Hard and soft coral gardens abound with schools of coral fish, pelagic marine life, mantas and turtles. Here are a few of the more famous dive sites with their descriptions, although there are many more spectacular sites around Pemba's smaller offshore islands.

Fundu Reef The visibility ranges from 20-40 m and there is a large sheer wall with overhangs and caverns. The coral is remarkable, especially the large rose coral and red and yellow sea fans. You can see many types of fish here including kingfish, triggerfish and wrasse. The reef is relatively shallow and therefore Fundu is a good spot for a first dive.

Kokota Reef Ideal for night diving, the waters are shallow and generally calmer, ranging from between 8-20 m. Of all the creatures that come out after dark, the Spanish dancer is a particular attraction.

Manta Point Visibility averages from between 20-40 m. Manta Point is one of the best sites in the world for close encounters with the giant manta rays that inhabit this area. The rays can be seen in groups of up to 15 and rise to depths as shallow as 9 m. The enormous variety of coral, fish and other marine life is so concentrated here you should try and include at least 2 dives. This is truly one of the finest dive sites in the region.

Mesali Island Visibility averages between 40-50 m. This is a wall dotted with small caves and ridges. Large rivers of sand run off the top of the reef to form wide canyons that enter the wall at approximately 25 m. Gorgonian fans are in abundance below 20 m and on a turning tide the marine life is exceptional and the currents strong. Giant grouper drift lazily through the reef and hundreds of surgeonfish cruise below divers.

Njao Gap Njao Gap is well known for its amazing wall diving. Mantas can be seen here in season and the coral is spectacular, but what distinguishes this particular location is the profusion of titan trigger-fish. Visibility varies from day to day, but is usually good to 30 m.

19th century describe the fortress as being rectangular, with two square and two round towers at the corners, topped by thatched roofs. Round towers are typical of the Arab and Swahili architecture of the time, but the square towers are unusual and indicate possible Portuguese influence. Construction of the old hospital destroyed all but the eastern corner and tower which now houses the Ministry of Women and Children. A battery, dating from the same period, overlooked the bay to the west, but only two cannons remain to mark the site. There are some handsome Moorish-style administrative buildings near the fort with verandas, and a **clock tower**. On the outskirts of town is a new hospital, built by the European Community overseas aid programme and a few kilometres past the old centre a huge new sports stadium, which is home to the local football team. The market and bus stand are both in the centre close to the mosque. There have been some strikes and riots during elections in recent years, as Pemba is the stronghold of the CUF opposition party.

Ruins at Pujini

About 10 km southeast of Chake Chake, this settlement is thought to date back to the 15th century. There was a fortified enclosure and rampart surrounded by a moat, the only known early fortification on the East Africa coast. It is believed to have been built by a particularly unpleasant character, nicknamed Mkame Ndume, which means 'a milker of men', because he worked his subjects so hard. He was known to order his servants to carry the large stones used to build the fortress whilst shuffling along on their buttocks. The memory remains and local people believe that the ruins are haunted. The settlement and the palace of Mkame Ndume were destroyed by the Portuguese when they arrived on the island in about 1520. Today the site is largely overgrown and there is little left of the fortications except for a crumbling staircase and some remains of 1 m thick walls. There are also the remnants of a two-chambered well that reputedly was used by the two wives of Ndume who lived in separate parts of the palace and never met. It is best to visit by hiring a bicycle (ask in Chake Chake).

Ruins at Ras Mkumbuu and Mesali Island

About 20 km west of Chake Chake, Ras Mkumbuu is probably Pemba's most important ruins, believed to date back about 1200 years, the oldest settlement south of Lamu Island in Kenya. It is the site of a settlement originating in the Shirazi period. The ruins include stone houses and pillar tombs and the remains of a 14th-century mosque. Of interest are the tombs decorated with pieces of porcelain that suggest an early connection with the Chinese. Most people visit by boat on the way to Mesali Island where the marine life on the reef make it excellent for diving and snorkelling and there is a fine beach. There are pleasant trails through the forest in the middle of the island which is rich in birdlife, and is also home to vervet monkeys and the Pemba flying fox (a large bat). Legend has it that the notorious 17th-century pirate Captain Kidd once had a hideout here and perhaps even buried some treasure during his stay. Dive schools regularly visit here on dives, and most of the lodges and guesthouses can arrange boat trips here.

Wete

This town is on the northwest coast of Pemba and serves as a port for the clove trade. It is a laid-back place on a hill overlooking the port with houses and small shops lining the main road down to the dhow harbour. Clustered close to the dock area is a pleasant group of colonial buildings. On the north side of the market a craftsman makes very fine carved doors. The town has a post office and police station and the *dala-dala* station is about halfway up the hill, *dala-dalas* to Chake Chake cost US$1.

The small island of **Mtabmwe Mkuu** opposite Wete, which means 'great arm of the sea', is linked to Pemba at low tide. It was once home to an 11th-century town and a number of silver coins have been discovered at the site, though there is nothing to see today and a small fishing village stands on the spot.

Tumbe and Konde

Tumbe is at the north end of Pemba and is a busy fishing village with a market where people from all around buy their fish in the mornings. Local fishermen contract to provide catches for firms, which chill the fish and export it to the mainland. At the end of the cool season in October, there is a boat race here. Teams of men compete, paddling dug-out canoes and the day is completed with a feast provided for contestants and onlookers. Konde is to the northeast of the island and is at the end of the tarmac road and the furthest most point of the *dala-dala* network. Access to Ngezi Forest is from here. There is no accommodation in Tumbe or Konde but both can be reached by *dala-dala* from Chake Chake.

Ngezi Forest Reserve

ⓘ *www.ngeziforest.or.tz, entrance fee US$3.*

The reserve covers 1440 ha and compromises ancient coastal forest that once covered all of Pemba. The area was declared a reserve in the 1950s after much of the island had been cleared for clove production. This is a thick blanket of forest with vines and creepers and a dense undergrowth that supports a variety of plants and wildlife. It has its own plant species and sub-species that are unique to this area. Most of the 27 species of bird recorded on Pemba have been spotted in the forest, some endemic to Pemba including hadada, the African goshawk, the palm-nut vulture, Scops owl, the malachite kingfisher and the Pemba white eye. Much of the ground is ancient coral rag, often sharp edged, containing pockets of soil. Mangrove forests grow on the tidal coastal creeks and the incoming tide sees seawater running deep upstream, forming brackish swampy areas. The central area contains heather dominated heathland where the soil is leached sand. The heather, *Philippia mafiensis*, is only found on Pemba and Mafia Islands.

Pemba's flying fox, a large fruit-eating bat, is found in Ngezi. Tree mammals include the Pemba vervet monkey and the Zanzibar red colobus monkey. Indolent-looking hyrax can also be seen climbing in the trees eating leaves. The Pemba blue duiker, an antelope about the size of a hare, is also here though it is very shy and is rarely spotted. Feral pigs, introduced long ago by the Portuguese, can be found along with the Javan civet cat, which was probably brought to the island by southeast Asian traders for the production of musk for perfume. The only endemic carnivore in Ngezi is the marsh mongoose, which normally lives by ponds and streams. There is a 2-km walking trail from the entrance that takes about an hour.

To the north of here is the secluded **Panga ya Watoro beach** on a peninsula that juts out from the island. At the end is the lighthouse at Ras Kigomasha, the far northwestern tip of the island; authorities are very sensitive so photography is not advised.

Pemba Island listings

For Sleeping and Eating price codes and other relevant information, see pages 12-17.

⊟ Sleeping

Mkoani *p113*

$$$$ Fundu Lagoon, north of Mkoani across the bay near the village of Wambaa and reached by boat organized by the resort (US$40), T0777-438668 (mob), www.fundulagoon.com. This luxury British-owned development is the top place to stay on Pemba. Very stylish, with 18 tented

rooms on stilts, overlooking a beautiful mangrove-fringed beach, and furnished with locally crafted hardwood furniture. 4 suites have private plunge pools and decks and are perfect for honeymooners. There's an infinity pool and spa, and all variety of watersports are available, including diving, sailing and windsurfing. 2 restaurants and 3 bars. Supports local communities through its Village Fund and has built a school for 500 children, installed several water wells and is planning a medical clinic. Bteween

US$305 and US$610 per person, depending on the room and season, this includes all meals and drinks. Recommended.

$ Jondeni Guest House, Mkoani overlooking the bay, T024-245 6042, T0777-460680 (mob), jondeniguest@hotmail.com. Rooms are simple but spotless with fans, nets and Zanzibari beds, some are en suite. Doubles from US$25-35, dorm beds US$10, including breakfast. The extremely friendly and helpful owner, Ali, serves good value meals and arranges local excursions including snorkelling at Mesali Bay, sailing, Wambaa village trips, sunset dhow cruises and canoeing. He can also arrange bike, motorbike and car hire. Internet available for guests. The garden has views of the bay and hammocks and loungers. Ali is planning to open 5 villas in Wambaa on the opposite side of the lagoon in Sep 2009.

Chake Chake p113

$$$ Pemba Paradise Beach and Resort, 7 km from Chake Chake near Vitongoji, T0763-444666 (mob) seif@pajebeachbungalows.com. This new lodge set in theMakoba Bay on the east coast is due to open in Jul 2009. There are 20 en suite rooms in bungalows, some overlooking the sea and each with their own small sunbathing area. Swimming pool and pool bar. Full board only for US$100 per person, which includes soft drinks but no alcohol. They can arrange transfers from the airport, diving and snorkelling, and excursions.

$$ Hamisa Village and Lodge, signposted on the left of the main road into Chake Chake if approaching from the north, T0754-015 148 (mob), hamisahotel@yahoo.com. About 500 m out of town, with 4 clean double rooms in bungalows. More are being built although work has currently stopped. There's a VIP room which is the same price as the doubles, even though it has a kitchen (not yet completed), a TV and a/c. The restaurant serves fresh fish and local food. Friendly staff.

$$ Pemba Clove Inn, Wesha Rd, Tibirinzi, about 500 m from town centre, T024-245 2795, pembacloveinn@zanzinet.com. By far the nicest place to stay in Chake Chake. 13 spotless rooms, with coconut wood beds, a/c, TVs, minibars and nets. Swimming pool and outdoor restaurant are planned for next year. Decent indoor restaurant. The friendly staff can arrange the usual island tours.

$$ Pemba Island Hotel, Wesha Rd, T0777-478464 (mob), www.pembaislandhotel.co.tz. There's nothing special about this hotel, rooms are fine and offer a/c, fans, nets and fridges, and there's a restaurant on the roof. Reception staff are unhelpful and there's a notice saying that guests must be indoors by 2200, with silence in the rooms until 0600.

$ Hotel La Tavern, opposite the People's Bank of Zanzibar, T024-245 2660. 4 spotlessly clean rooms, nets and towels are provided, some rooms with own bathrooms. Evening meals are available if pre-ordered.

Wete p115

$ Pemba Crown Hotel, Wete Main Rd, T0777-429208 (mob), T0777-493667 (mob), sales@pembacrown.com. All 13 rooms have a/c, fans, mosquito nets, TVs and en suite bathrooms. They're clean and in a handy location for the market and bus stand. Dinner must be pre-ordered. Doubles US$35, singles US$25 including breakfast.

$ Sharook Guest House, near the market and bus stand, down the track that leads to the harbour, T024-245 4386, sharookguest house@yahoo.com. Run by a friendly guy called Suleiman, it's very simple but clean, and has a restaurant with the best food in town, though it has to be pre-ordered. Own generator. Can arrange excursions, snorkelling trips to local islands and bicycle hire.

$ Sharook 2, on the road to the port, take the road opposite the **Pemba Crown Hotel**, and it's on the left about 10 m up a small track. Also owned by Suleiman and with the same contact details as above. There are 8 rooms

Clove production

It has been estimated that there are about 6 million clove trees on the islands of Zanzibar and Pemba and they cover about one-tenth of the land area. The plantations are found mainly in the west and northwest of the islands where the soil is deeper and the landscape hillier. To the east the soil is less deep and fertile and is known as 'coral landscape'.

Cloves were at one time only grown in the Far East and they were greatly prized. On his first trip back from the East, Vasco da Gama took a cargo back to Portugal and they were later introduced by the French to Mauritius and then to Zanzibar by Sayyid Said who was the first Arab Sultan. At this time all the work was done by slaves who enabled the plantations to be established and clove production to become so important to the economy of the islands. When the slaves were released and labour was no longer free, some of the plantations found it impossible to survive although production did continue and Zanzibar remained at the head of the world's clove production.

Cloves are actually the unopened buds of the clove tree. They grow in clusters and must be picked when the buds are full but before they actually open. They are collected in sprays and the buds are then picked off before being spread on the ground to dry out. They are spread out on mats made from woven coconut palm fronds for about five days, turned over regularly so that they dry evenly – the quicker they dry the better the product.

There may be many clove trees on Zanzibar now – but there were even more in the past. In 1872 a great hurricane destroyed many of the trees and it was after this that Pemba took over from Zanzibar as the largest producer. Zanzibar, however, has retained the role of chief seller and exporter of cloves so the Pemba cloves go to Zanzibar before being sold on.

here, all gleaming new and clean, all en suite. Zanzibari beds, fans and nets. Suleiman is planning a rooftop restaurant (partially) overlooking Fundu Island and an internet café on the ground floor. Reports welcome.

Ngezi Forest Reserve p116
$$$ **Kervan Saray Beach**, near Makangale Village, T0773-176737 (mob), www.kervan saraybeach.com. The new home of **Swahili Divers** (see Activities and tours, below), and primarily a diving centre with accommodation, although there's plenty here for non-divers too. A very chilled lodge in lovely gardens, with an open restaurant and bar/lounge area, and a new swimming pool opening in autumn 2009. The 11 clean and spacious rooms are in 6 bungalows, have traditional *barazza* beds, mosquito nets with fans inside, and private bathrooms. US$140 per person full board, and there's a dorm room with 3 bunk beds for US$45 per person. Also offer some excellent packages such as 6 nights' full board with 5 days diving for US$1250 per person sharing or US$850 with dorm accommodation. Excursions, including forest walks into the nearby Ngezi Reserve, sea kayaking, fishing, and airport transfers.

Panga ya Watoro Beach
$$$$ **The Manta Resort** (formerly **Manta Reef Lodge**), in the extreme northwest of the island, T0777-511293 (mob), www.themanta resort.com. Quiet and wonderfully remote location on a cliff overlooking a private beach, the lodge has a large central area with terrace, veranda, lounge, restaurant and snooker room. 20 en suite double rooms

in individual cottages, some with sea view, all attractively decorated. New swimming pool and beach bar, and snorkelling, kayaking, game fishing can be arranged. Also has a dive centre.

🍴 Eating

Many of the places listed under Sleeping have restaurants, see above.

Chake Chake p113
🍴 **Balloon Bros**, just south of the market and bus stand and opposite the mosque on main street. Charcoal grill, cold drinks, pleasant patio with thatched bandas to sit under.

🏔 Activities and tours

Pemba Island p111
Diving
To appreciate Pemba's magical diversity fully, take the liveaboard option and dive the east coast, for this is the territory of the schooling hammerheads. For more information on diving Pemba, see page .
Dive 7/10, Fundu Lagoon, T024-223 2926, www.fundulagoon.com. Luxury outfit.
The Manta Resort, see Sleeping. Luxury.
Swahili Divers, Kervan Saray Beach, T0773-176738 (mob), www.swahilidivers.com. 5-star PADI Gold Palm Resort dive centre. Dive on the east and west coast of Pemba and during Feb-May, head for the southern coast for the migrating whale sharks. Single dives cost US$80, doubles US$130 and 3 dives US$180, plus US$30 for equipment hire. Have very reasonable diving packages for residents

at their lodge, see Sleeping, page 118). Day guests can be picked up at Konde if they arrive by *dala-dala* by 0800. PADI courses available, including Discover Scuba, Open Water, Advanced, Rescue Diver, Dive Master. Highly recommended for budget travellers.

Tour operators
Most hotels and guesthouses can arrange excursions. Ali at **Jondeni Guesthouse** (see Sleeping, page 117) is keen to show travellers that Pemba has lots to offer, and is very helpful.
Faizin Tours, near the bank, Mkoani, T024-223 0705. Ferry tickets and tours of the island.

🚌 Transport

Pemba Island p111
Air
Coastal Air, T024-2452162, Pemba Airport, flies to **Dar** daily at 1635 (50 mins, US$121). To **Zanzibar** at 1640 (30 mins, US$101). To **Tanga** at 1515 (25 mins, US$75).
    Zanair fly daily to **Zanzibar** at 1045, 1500, 1645 (US$101).

Ferry
The quickest ferry is **Sepiddeh**, T0713-282 365, which departs Pemba to **Zanzibar** and **Dar**, Wed-Mon at 1300. 1st class costs US$60, economy US$55. To Zanzibar 1st class costs US$40 and economy US$35.
    Sea Express, T024-211 0217, operates a ferry to **Dar** on Mon and Thu, and runs between Pemba and **Zanzibar** at 1300. See also Dar es Salaam transport, page 52.

Contents

Footnotes

Index

Titles available in the Footprint *Focus* range

Latin America	UK RRP	US RRP
Bahia & Salvador	£7.99	$11.95
Buenos Aires & Pampas	£7.99	$11.95
Costa Rica	£8.99	$12.95
Cuzco, La Paz & Lake Titicaca	£8.99	$12.95
El Salvador	£5.99	$8.95
Guadalajara & Pacific Coast	£6.99	$9.95
Guatemala	£8.99	$12.95
Guyana, Guyane & Suriname	£5.99	$8.95
Havana	£6.99	$9.95
Honduras	£7.99	$11.95
Nicaragua	£7.99	$11.95
Paraguay	£5.99	$8.95
Quito & Galápagos Islands	£7.99	$11.95
Recife & Northeast Brazil	£7.99	$11.95
Rio de Janeiro	£8.99	$12.95
São Paulo	£5.99	$8.95
Uruguay	£6.99	$9.95
Venezuela	£8.99	$12.95
Yucatán Peninsula	£6.99	$9.95

Asia	UK RRP	US RRP
Angkor Wat	£5.99	$8.95
Bali & Lombok	£8.99	$12.95
Chennai & Tamil Nadu	£8.99	$12.95
Chiang Mai & Northern Thailand	£7.99	$11.95
Goa	£6.99	$9.95
Hanoi & Northern Vietnam	£8.99	$12.95
Ho Chi Minh City & Mekong Delta	£7.99	$11.95
Java	£7.99	$11.95
Kerala	£7.99	$11.95
Kolkata & West Bengal	£5.99	$8.95
Mumbai & Gujarat	£8.99	$12.95

Africa	UK RRP	US RRP
Beirut	£6.99	$9.95
Damascus	£5.99	$8.95
Durban & KwaZulu Natal	£8.99	$12.95
Fès & Northern Morocco	£8.99	$12.95
Jerusalem	£8.99	$12.95
Johannesburg & Kruger National Park	£7.99	$11.95
Kenya's beaches	£8.99	$12.95
Kilimanjaro & Northern Tanzania	£8.99	$12.95
Zanzibar & Pemba	£7.99	$11.95

Europe	UK RRP	US RRP
Bilbao & Basque Region	£6.99	$9.95
Granada & Sierra Nevada	£6.99	$9.95
Málaga	£5.99	$8.95
Orkney & Shetland Islands	£5.99	$8.95
Skye & Outer Hebrides	£6.99	$9.95

North America	UK RRP	US RRP
Vancouver & Rockies	£8.99	$12.95

Australasia	UK RRP	US RRP
Brisbane & Queensland	£8.99	$12.95
Perth	£7.99	$11.95

For the latest books, e-books and smart phone app releases, and a wealth of travel information, visit us at:
www.footprinttravelguides.com.

footprinttravelguides.com

Join us on facebook for the latest travel news, product releases, offers and amazing competitions: www.facebook.com/footprintbooks.com.